100
20TH -
CENTURY
GARDENS &
LANDSCAPES

100 20TH - CENTURY GARDENS & LANDSCAPES

Edited by
Susannah Charlton
and Elain Harwood

BATSFORD

First published in the United Kingdom in 2020 by Batsford
43 Great Ormond Street
London WC1N 3HZ

An imprint of Pavilion Books Group

ISBN: 9781849945295

A CIP catalogue record for this book is available from the British Library.

10 9 8 7 6 5 4 3 2 1

Reproduction by Mission Productions, Hong Kong
Printed by Toppan Leefung Printing Ltd, China

This book can be ordered direct from the publisher at the website:
www.pavilionbooks.com or try your local bookshop.

PAGE 2 Hemel Water
Gardens, Hertfordshire

CONTENTS

FOREWORD

100 20th-Century Gardens & Landscapes gives an overview of the radical changes that have taken place in the landscapes that surround us during the past century, both in how they were created and how we use them. It is both a history and a celebration. The Twentieth Century Society is primarily focused on buildings, but we work to protect landscapes too, especially where they were planned together with buildings as a complete ensemble. We are a conservation organisation, and landscapes offer different challenges to buildings. While a building is usually deemed complete when the builders leave site, gardens are planned to grow and develop; the intended final effect may only be achieved many years later, when plants and trees have had time to mature. Some elements can run wild, others decay. What does this mean for restoration objectives? To what state should a restoration aim to return a landscape to? And to what extent do we see gradual changes as part of a natural process akin to the patination of building fabric?

Landscapes are even more vulnerable to redevelopment pressures than buildings, be it complete redevelopment, or infilling spaces between buildings for financial gain or to accommodate a growing organisation. Neglect or lack of maintenance can have a major impact far more quickly than a similar disregard for a relatively robust building. Planting has also to evolve, to cope with changing uses and the changing climate.

Statutory consultees, like the Twentieth Century Society and the Gardens Trust, can often only intervene to save a landscape at the eleventh hour when it is under imminent threat. Many excellent designed landscapes may not meet the demanding criteria for registration by Historic England, and need protection by other means. Measures such as covenants to protect the landscape, as used at the Span estates or Hampstead Garden Suburb, can better help to maintain the planting and character of shared green space and streetscapes. Perhaps even more important is that people understand and appreciate the everyday landscapes around them. We hope this book will spur you to visit this very diverse group of places, some of which may not initially appear to be the work of designers at all.

The Twentieth Century Society is a tiny organisation facing growing demand for the conservation advice, research and campaigning that we undertake, as more of the heritage we champion comes under threat. Please join our many members, who enable us to protect outstanding 20th-century buildings and landscapes.

Catherine Croft
www.c20society.org.uk

RIGHT Span Estate at Templemere, Surrey

INTRODUCTION

It was once obvious what constituted a garden or a landscape. There were the grandiose private gardens of the wealthy and/or privileged, and for the rest of us there were public parks and squares laid out by municipal authorities. Or so it seemed until the 20th century.

Grand gardens continued to be formed, but many more people now had their own plot, however small, to create a significant outdoor space or 'garden room', as Thomas Church and John Brookes described urban gardens. Many more varied public spaces began to be created, ranging from the poignant war memorial or crematorium garden, to those that celebrated a festival, the Millennium, or – more enigmatically – the world's hopes for peace. Landscaping became a wider part of the public realm, especially after World War II. New towns, housing estates, universities, reservoirs and motorways – even new forests – were planned to look good as well as to serve their users, so that the hand of mankind has a hold over the landscape everywhere we go in town and country today. This diversity and the importance of landscape reflects the egalitarianism and optimism that were so important to all that was good about the 20th century.

The most distinguished and significant of these gardens and landscapes deserve to be understood, appreciated and protected as an important record of British life, just as much as the gardens and landscapes of earlier centuries.

In many cases, they form part of a complete ensemble with significant post-1914 buildings, either because they were designed at the same time, in collaboration with the architect, or because they constitute an important context for that architecture.

The Twentieth Century Society campaigns to protect landscapes as well as buildings. This is easy to explain where buildings and their landscape form an ensemble. It is more challenging when the landscape is a subtle streetscape or park that we take for granted with benign indifference, yet is an important part of the designed landscape. Public landscapes do not have the protection of a wealthy owner with the long-term vision and resources to help them survive for the future. Townscapes are particularly subject to the relentless pressures of austerity Britain, from council maintenance cuts to commercial redevelopment or privatisation, which reduce the sense of communal ownership of landscapes designed for public good. Even when their significance is recognised, well-meaning incremental changes – intrusive safety rails, excessive signage, inappropriate sculpture or new planting – can erode the quality of the very design they were supposed to protect or enhance.

As land values rise, the speed of demolition increases, especially in the commercial sector when changing ownership, obsolete facilities or the need to expand exert

RIGHT Hauser & Wirth, Somerset

powerful financial pressures. The RMC head office in Surrey with its 'exceptionally accomplished and richly detailed landscape design combining courtyards and rooftop gardens' was threatened with demolition just 25 years after its completion in 1990. Thankfully this has been saved, and in 2019 the Society was able to get not just one, but three listings for the Pearl Assurance headquarters outside Peterborough: the building at Grade II, the war memorial at Grade II*, and the 25 acres (10ha) of landscaped grounds registered at Grade II. The grounds were designed by Professor Arnold Weddle, whose highly creative re-working of a familiar formal language complements the post-modern design of the Pearl Centre. However, the listed Bird's Eye offices in Walton-on-Thames, with landscaping by Phillip Hicks, was demolished in 2019. Despite our sustained objections, the beautifully executed essay in modernist landscape that was designed by architects Robert Matthew, Johnson-Marshall & Partners with planting by Sylvia Crowe for the Commonwealth Institute in London was delisted and demolished when the building was redeveloped in 2015–16 for the Design Museum. This shows how vulnerable even a registered landscape can be if the local authority and Historic England do not ensure that it has the robust protection it deserves.

Protecting significant private gardens can be equally difficult, dependent on sympathetic owners with the skills and resources to honour the original design and planting. Preben Jakobsen designed a rare private garden for No.5 Pipers Green Lane in Edgware, Middlesex, the blueprint for his influential Sculpture Garden at the 1982 Chelsea Flower Show. Now, sadly, only the pool remains from his original design. The Gardens Trust have been leading work to propose significant 20th-century gardens and designed landscapes for addition to the Register of Parks and Gardens before they are lost for good, and the Twentieth Century Society has supported this campaign.

Gardens present particular conservation challenges, as trees and plants are constantly changing and must be carefully managed and renewed. Even a well-maintained garden can lose its soul unless its guardians capture the spirit of the original gardener, as Penelope Hobhouse did so successfully with the garden created by Phyllis Reiss at Tintinhull. Gardeners tend to be conservative, with the influence of Gertrude Jekyll (1843–1932), whose book on *Colour in the Flower Garden* is still consulted, and William Robinson (1838–1935), advocate of cottage plants and wild gardens, extending through much of the 20th century. There were some pioneering modernist gardens, like that by Christopher Tunnard for St Ann's Court, but it was not until the 1970s that the idea of the garden as an outdoor room, with a more formal design and low-maintenance, architectural planting became popular,

LEFT Rutland Water, Rutland (top); Sissinghurst Castle, Kent (bottom)

thanks to John Brookes's highly influential book *The Room Outside* (1969), which inspired many television garden makeover programmes.

Many of the country's best-known 20th century gardens were designed around much older buildings. This book includes some of the most famous, such as Sissinghurst and Great Dixter, but our focus has been on gardens and landscapes that were created to complement buildings or developments of the same period.

Early in the century, public parks, like private gardens, were planted with extravagant and colourful bedding schemes, which served as symbols of civic pride and helped seaside resorts to compete for visitors. Yet the Venetian Waterways in Great Yarmouth also provided relief work for unemployed men during the depression in the 1920s, foreshadowing the way that festival gardens were commissioned to regenerate depressed areas like Liverpool and Sunderland in the 1980s. Annual bedding displays that were once taken for granted require what now seem like extravagant amounts of maintenance and watering: local authorities can no longer afford civic display and nor can the environment. The emphasis in recent parks has been on sustainable planting that can be maintained by the community, as at Dalston Eastern Curve garden, which incorporates vegetable beds, children's activities and a café, making it a popular local hub.

The pressing need for more housing can make it hard to win the argument for conservation, particularly when councils are looking to increase the density of low-rise estates of social housing designed with striking landscape settings, like Cressingham Gardens or the Alton Estate in London. The gardens of Highpoint, Berthold Lubetkin's two Grade I-listed blocks of private flats in Highgate, may not themselves be at immediate risk, but the highly desirable land around them is certainly under pressure for development. This could be hugely damaging to such an important site, described by John Allan as 'the most complete realisation of a particular urban planning model – compact apartments in a recreational landscape offering an idealised vision of modern living'.

The threat to natural landscapes from changes required by the pressures of public access and health and safety requirements is widely acknowledged. Designed landscapes are just as vulnerable to these pressures, yet their fragility is not as widely discussed. In 2004 the Twentieth Century Society objected to plans to erect handrails at Portmeirion in Wales, which would have been totally counter to the picturesque aesthetic of an Italianate seaside village that Clough Williams-Ellis created with his holiday centre.

The last 100 years have seen both the emergence of landscape architecture as a distinct profession and the popularisation of garden design. The Institute of Landscape Architects (now the Landscape Institute) was founded in 1929 and brought to prominence specialist landscape designers such as Geoffrey Jellicoe, Brenda Colvin, Sylvia Crowe and Preben Jakobsen, whose work forms the backbone of this book. However, in the 21st century it seems that many developers are unwilling to invest in the skills of landscape professionals or in providing generous green space for new housing. The landscapes in this book make an eloquent case for the value of involving landscape architects in their conservation, and in new developments, just as they were central to the creation of the new towns and universities of the 1950s and 1960s. By combining the domestic, industrial, civic and commercial we hope this book will encourage people to see the designed landscapes around them with new eyes and value them, just as we treasure more traditional parks and gardens.

Susannah Charlton

LEFT Alton Estate, Roehampton

1914–
1929

Otley Hall

Location: Otley, Suffolk
Designed by: Francis Inigo Thomas,
Sylvia Landsberg and Simon Nickson
Created: 1915–2009

New owner Mrs Sherston commissioned a garden plan for this 16th-century manor house from Inigo Thomas in 1915. The death of her husband in World War I meant that it was not implemented until the 1980s, when two stew ponds were joined by a canal to form an H shape. The spoil was used to create a viewing mound to the west.

In 1997 Sylvia Landsberg was commissioned by the next owner, Nicholas Hagger, to add Tudor features including a knot garden, herber and vine-and-rose tunnel. Later a small orchard of apple, pear and mulberry was planted and a flowery mead, designed by Simon Nickson. This combines formal avenues of yew surrounded by wildflowers and grasses. Nickson also created a mown grass labyrinth in 2009, based on that in the nave of Chartres Cathedral. The garden exemplifies the rediscovery of historic garden styles, beautifully complementing the house and its resident white peacock.

Susannah Charlton

Brookwood Cemetery

Location: Woking, Surrey
Designed by: Commonwealth War
Graves Commission
Created: 1917
Registered: Grade I

Brookwood Cemetery is the largest cemetery in the UK, the vastness of which can be appreciated from the London–Basingstoke train line that runs along its northern edge. Established as the London Necropolis in 1852, its importance as a 20th-century landscape lies in Brookwood Military Cemetery that forms part of it. The largest site of the Commonwealth War Graves Commission, it holds 1,752 graves from both world wars in sections organised by the nationality of those lost, both from the Commonwealth countries and countries including France, Poland and Czechoslovakia. There is also a separate American cemetery by Egerton Swartwout that contains 468 graves. There are some fine individual buildings across the site and the landscaping and care of each area shows, in a smaller scale, the manner in which different nations designed for their war dead: Edward Maufe's restrained Air Forces shelter building contrasting with the highly decorative Beaux-Arts chapel by Swartwout in the American Cemetery.

Jon Wright

Port Lympne

Location: Hythe, Kent
Designed by: Sir Philip Sassoon
and Philip Tilden
Created: 1918
Registered: Grade II*

Peter Stansky's lively biography of the Sassoon siblings offers a stream of adjectives for Philip Sassoon: 'exotic', 'unstuffy', 'new world', 'idiosyncratic', 'one of the most exciting, tantalizing personalities of the age'. All this is true also of the garden he created at Port Lympne, where with the help of Philip Tilden, he turned his disappointing Herbert Baker villa into the dazzling centrepiece of the last word in extravagant inter-war landscapes.

The grounds, designed mostly by Tilden, assisted by Norah Lindsay, were divided into compartments for terraces, thematic planting of various kinds, a water garden, swimming pools-de-luxe and much more. Wide mixed borders, enclosed by tall clipped cypresses, were replanted by Russell Page around 1974. But its glory is the surviving 125-step Trojan Stair that cascades towards a breathtaking view of Romney Marsh and the English Channel. The Doric temples at its summit have gone: but what remains testifies to an extraordinary, vivid personality.

Timothy Brittain-Catlin

Papworth Village Settlement

Location: Ermine Street, Cambridgeshire
Designed by: Dr Pendrill Varrier-Jones
Created: 1919

Set in 50 acres (20.32ha) of spacious parkland at Papworth Hall, this pioneering village for tuberculosis sufferers had sanatorium wings for men and women, but also, to avoid the harm caused by idleness, included light industrial workshops, education and recreation facilities. It also had 'living quarters for life' for patients and their families. After initial medical treatment, patients moved first into open-air, 7ft (2.1m) square huts with pyramidal felt roofs in nearby meadows, surrounded by mature trees, and then into prettily gardened communal bungalows.

Finally, their families came to live with them in the cottages, where patients slept outside on verandahs and tended their own gardens. Its success inspired other such colonies. In 1936 Walter Gropius and Maxwell Fry were commissioned to design a new school but sadly it was never built. By 1947, on the eve of TB's eradication, Papworth could accommodate 350 patients and 200 ex-patients and their families; it is now the Royal Papworth Hospital.

Imogen Magnus

Snowshill Manor Garden

Location: Near Broadway, Worcestershire
Designed by: Charles Paget Wade and Mackay Hugh Baillie Scott
Created: 1919
Registered: Grade II

In 1919 architect and antique collector Charles Paget Wade bought near-derelict 16th-century Snowshill Manor and 14 acres (5.67ha) of land, restoring the manor to house his collections. Both house and garden design were attributed to Wade, but in 1980 *Country Life* reported that a letter and garden plan among Wade's papers 'proved conclusively' that Arts and Crafts architect Baillie Scott had designed the garden.

An immense flight of steps leading down from the house, bordered by a yew colonnade, forms the backbone of the garden. It was constructed as a series of terraces enclosed by walls to create garden rooms, often centred on a decorative element, such as a wellhead or sundial, while existing ponds and streams allowed the creation of small water features. Photographs by Wade show the garden rooms simply planted with lawns, narrow flower borders and climbing plants. In 1951, five years before his death, Wade presented Snowshill Manor to the National Trust.

Barbara Simms

Welwyn
Garden City

Location: Hertfordshire
Designed by: Louis de Soissons
Created: 1920

Founded by Ebenezer Howard in 1919, Welwyn epitomises his concept of a 'marriage of town and country'. De Soissons masterminded the overall plan and landscaping in 1920, retaining existing trees and selecting over 100 new species.

The formal Beaux-Arts town centre has two wide roads with central planting, including double avenues of lime trees separating people from traffic: Parkway has lawns and rose beds underplanted with lavender, catmint and geraniums, while Howardsgate has double herbaceous borders. An elegant coronation fountain was added in 1953. To the north, the campus comprises 4.5 acres (1.82ha) of trees and lawns. The scheme gives views on a grand scale, with Lombardy poplars, not buildings, providing height.

In contrast, much of the housing is laid out in intimate closes with narrow roads, open front gardens, hedges and distinctive trees, giving a countryside feel. One, for example, was planted with purple leaf plum, golden maple and mountain ash, another with silver birch and red maple.

Angela Eserin

Clacton Seafront Gardens

Location: Clacton, Essex
Designed by: Daniel Bowe
Created: 1921, altered 1924
Registered: Grade II

Post-war guidebooks sold Clacton as the 'Town of a Thousand Gardens.' The most quintessentially seaside ones were laid out by county surveyor Daniel Bowe to beautify the cliff-top strip between road and promenade. With inter-war resorts in competition for longest sunshine hours and best outdoor attractions, these gardens represented an intensification of the Victorian habit of tidying up the coastal edge with manicured lawns and formal bedding.

Clacton's seafront gardens were restored in the late 1990s but survive largely as they were created. The bedding patterns around Charles Hartwell's 1924 war memorial are contemporary with it, as are the structural cordylines that give height among the annuals.

Westwards from the pier the 1921 sunken rose and flower gardens lead to two level compartments with crazy paving, now planted with Mediterranean and sensory themes. Between them, three pavilions of different, yet pleasingly similar, design provide sheltered seats to enjoy the garden and sea views.

Kathryn Ferry

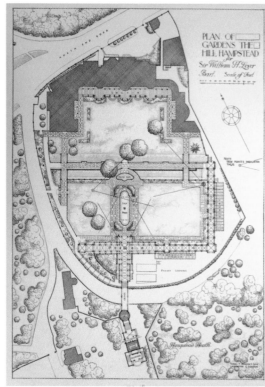

The Hill
(Inverforth House)

Location: Hampstead, London
Designed by: Thomas H. Mawson & Sons
Created: 1922
Registered: Grade II*

Mawson designed an extraordinary garden at The Hill with a demanding brief and a difficult site. He had worked on previous projects for his client, the industrialist William Lever, 1st Viscount Leverhulme, who had bought the property in 1904. In a little over 3 acres (1.21ha) on steeply sloping ground, Mawson had to conceive a way of hiding the garden from people on Hampstead Heath, while keeping the sweeping outward views open. He juxtaposed spaces for lavish entertaining with a gardeners' working area. Using soil excavated from digging the Northern Underground line and building high retaining walls, Mawson designed a formal garden of terraces, lily pond and lawns around the house, and an elevated pergola walk built in three phases between 1906 and 1922. The garden suffered badly in the 1987 storm, which led to a magnificent restoration of the garden and pergola when the gardens were reunited in the ownership of the City of London.

Camilla Beresford

Highfields and University of Nottingham

Location: University Boulevard, Nottingham
Designed by: Percy Morley Horder (Highfields) and Geoffrey Jellicoe (University of Nottingham masterplan)
Created: 1922–55
Registered: Grade II (Highfields)

In 1919 the chemist Sir Jesse Boot purchased Highfields and two other villas of around 1800. He proposed a model factory and village, but when American shareholders objected he created a public park, gifted to the city in 1932. On the rising land behind he built a campus for Nottingham, a university college, opened in 1928 and raised to university status in 1948.

Horder extended Highfields's fishpond as a boating lake, with gardens, bowls and croquet lawns, all dominated by his Trent Building (1922–28). Public park and university college were visually linked but physically separate. The university bought more villas to the north after 1948. In 1955 it commissioned a masterplan from Jellicoe, who proposed an arts building in botanical gardens, a circular assembly hall and a perimeter road. The clean rolls of Cripps Hill indicate his hand but Donald McMorran was preferred for the buildings and a revised road plan. Existing villa gardens were linked by new conifer planting and a wildflower meadow. A flower garden was created to celebrate the Millennium.

Elain Harwood

Stanley Park

Location: West Park Drive, Blackpool, Lancashire

Designed by: Thomas H. Mawson & Sons

Created: 1922

Registered: Grade II*

Blackpool's Stanley Park is part of an ambitious town-planning scheme designed by Thomas Mawson and published in 1922. The park was funded by the development of the surrounding streets, and enclosed by a road called Park Drive. It was carefully planned to relate to the existing roads and the town centre nearly a mile (1.5km) to the south-west. It opened in 1926.

The park incorporated not only Italianate and rose gardens, pergolas and lakeside terraces at its centre but also sports facilities including bowling greens, football and tennis courts, a golf course and a running track, now a sports centre (built in 1994). It contains a delightful Art Deco cafeteria built in 1937 to a design by C.J. Robinson, on the site of what Mawson planned as a 'Social Centre'. In the early 2000s the park was subject to a £5m restoration funded by the Heritage Lottery Fund and the council, which saw the repair of the Mawson infrastructure.

David Lambert

Ramsgate from E. Cliff. 1744. N. & Co. Ltd

Winterstoke Gardens

Location: Victoria Parade, East Cliff, Ramsgate, Kent
Designed by: Sir John Burnet & Partners
Created: 1923

Early 20th-century seaside resorts jealously vied for a share of holidaymakers' increasing leisure time and disposable income. Ramsgate renewed itself by laying on new attractions, smartening up its seafront and constructing new routes to the cliffs. Dame Janet Stancomb-Wills (1854–1932), the town's first woman mayor, funded Winterstoke Gardens on the town's East Cliff and commissioned Sir John Burnet to design it.

Laid out by James Pulham & Son, the garden is terraced, with a band of Pulhamite rockery separating lawns and ornamental ponds from a lower cliff-top promenade. Built into the rockwork is a central sun shelter with a curved Tuscan colonnade. Set within was Gilbert Bayes's punning sculpture of children playing with a ram, now sadly lost. The sun shelter is crowned with a heraldic shield, also by Bayes, depicting a similar subject in relief.

Geraint Franklin

Dartington Hall

Location: Near Totnes, Devon
Designed by: Beatrix Farrand and Percy Cane
Created: 1925
Registered: Grade II*

In 1925, Leonard and Dorothy Elmhirst bought the Dartington estate, with its semi-derelict medieval and Tudor courtyard buildings, to start a progressive school and to farm productively, as a showcase for rural regeneration. Dorothy inherited the Whitney US rail-building fortune, and was a patron of artists, craftsmen and garden designers. The Garden Department at Dartington employed 50 people in 1934.

With its terraced Tilt Yard, steep hillside and backdrop of mature trees, the 38 acres (15.37ha) of garden around the Hall developed incrementally, first with the American Beatrix Farrand, focusing on shrubs, magnolias, yew, bay and holly along woodland paths, succeeded post-war by the English Percy Cane, who cleared a glade from the western boundary, with a classical temple designed by Robert Hening. Dorothy herself provided the continuity, at work in a large blue hat whenever she could spare the time. The gardens are being sensitively re-worked to a masterplan by Dan Pearson.

Alan Powers

THE PRIVATE GARDEN IN THE 20TH CENTURY

By the last few decades of the 19th century garden designers and homeowners had turned away from the brightly coloured bedding of the High Victorian era to more natural planting, as promoted by William Robinson and Gertrude Jekyll. Jekyll believed that a garden should be in keeping with a house's architecture and that iincorporate features, such as a lawn, herbaceous border, rose garden, dry stone wall, formal pool and a croquet or tennis lawn, laid out as garden rooms. This garden style was inspired by the earlier teachings of John Ruskin and William Morris, based on a rediscovery of nature and English traditions and looking back to the medieval period. An 'opposing' group of architects, led by Reginald Blomfield and John Dando Sedding, believed that a house and garden should be an architectural whole and more formal in style, often imitating Jacobean gardens. The controversy between the two groups was partly solved by Jekyll with the architect Edwin Lutyens, their gardens combining geometric design and hard landscaping in local materials and exuberant planting that became characteristic of the 'Arts and Crafts' or Edwardian garden style.

Due to economic pressures, the years before World War I were the last period of great house and garden building: Lutyens only built three country houses after 1918 and Blomfield remembered in his memoirs, 'that delightful country house practice which I was lucky enough to have built up before the war, and which since the war has ceased to exist'. The war left many country houses and their gardens in a state of neglect, but there were still sufficient wealthy clients to provide commissions for architects and interior designers, and in the garden the socialite Norah Lindsay drew out garden plans 'with the tip of her umbrella'. New gardens were often created or developed around old houses, most notably by the American Lawrence Johnston at Hidcote Manor, Gloucestershire, and Vita Sackville-West and Harold Nicolson at Sissinghurst Castle, Kent. These gardens featured 'green architecture' (neatly clipped yew hedges, plants trained as standards and topiary); wisteria and roses tumbling over pergolas; plants growing through steps and exuberant borders. Such plant-oriented gardens are well documented, but what of the four million new houses and gardens built in England between the wars?

Before World War I only about ten per cent of homes were owner occupied, but this increased dramatically post-war. Many new homes were for rent on local authority estates, but those who could afford to buy looked to private suburban developments on the countryside fringes. Advertisements exploited the aspirations of potential customers, enticing young couples to 'small, labour-saving houses with garages and gardens' in leafy suburbs 'where you will have room to breathe'. The model for gardens of all sizes in the early post-war years was Jekyll's *Gardens*

RIGHT Hidcote Manor, Gloucestershire

for Small Country Houses, first published in 1912 but reprinted six times before 1927. Although such 'nostalgic' gardens were the most popular, in 1929 Richard Sudell, *Ideal Home's* gardening editor, encouraged new ideas: 'The modernist spirit has extended to the garden. People… ask for something new – something better.' In contrast, the talks of radio gardener Mr Middleton promoted a traditional country lifestyle: 'A perfect lawn, a crazy path and a rockery, pretty trees and shrubs, a rose arbour and flowers galore; fresh lettuces and tomatoes for tea.' Why were English gardeners reluctant to break with the past, unlike those in mainland Europe?

The few attempts to rethink garden design were inspired by the Modern Movement. Function was the keyword – to make design appropriate to the 'spirit of the age'. In a 1925 Paris exhibition, a few designers had applied developments in the fine and applied arts to the garden, the most celebrated being Gabriel Guevrekian's 'Garden of Water and Light', inspired by the forms of cubism. Such gardens, however, were more like sculptures than designs, using the new understanding of space. The opportunity to design homes with freely flowing space allowed increased contact between the inside and the outside. The Swiss architect Le Corbusier proposed white, liner-like houses with roof gardens, providing fresh air and light and space for leisure activities. The garden was seen as a foil to the

building, a 'Virgilian landscape' reminiscent of the 18th century landscape garden, as at the Villa Savoye (1929–31) just outside Paris. Was this then the type of garden to complement revolutionary ideas for house design in Britain?

The balconies and roof gardens of such modernist houses appeared austere to the British and not conducive to family activities. More acceptable were the 'gardens for people', promoted by Christopher Tunnard after his visit to the Stockholm Exhibition in 1930 and published in his book *Gardens in the Modern Landscape* (1938). Tunnard's project at Bentley Wood, East Sussex, with the architect Serge Chermayeff included a terrace with flowerbeds and a rectangular lily pool, a view of the Downs being framed by a partly glazed wooden trellis. A Henry Moore garden form (*Recumbent Figure,* 1938) sited on a plinth at the far end of the terrace displayed sculpture in a new way, as 'a mediator between modern house and ageless land'. A photograph of Mrs Chermayeff relaxing on the terrace documents it as a 'place for living', an outdoor room.

New ideas were published in *Landscape and Garden*, the journal of the Institute of Landscape Architects (formed in 1929). Prominent members, such as Brenda Colvin, Sylvia Crowe, Peter Shepheard and Geoffrey Jellicoe, promoted the small private garden as 'an extension of the house… a place to live in and should be designed primarily for that purpose'. In California, Thomas Church encouraged people

LEFT Villa Savoye, Poissy (top); Bentley Wood, East Sussex (bottom)

to create gardens they wanted 'rather than those they think they should have', publishing his ideas in *Gardens are for People* (1955). He was a promoter of 'the integration of the house and garden' and 'indoor-outdoor living' but rarely used the term 'outdoor room'. This became part of post-war popular vocabulary through the writings of garden and landscape designer John Brookes.

Brookes was keen to adapt the idea of the outside room to the needs of the British homeowner. His early work in the 1960s focused on gardens in fashionable areas of London, such as Chelsea, Kensington and St John's Wood, where land values were high and gardens small. Standard features appeared in these designs: overlapping squares to create a 'zig-zag' movement, dark blue-grey Kentstone paving, white gravel chippings, white trelliswork, colour-washed walls and a pergola to create a formal outdoor space adjoining the building. In 1969 Brookes published *Room Outside: A New Approach to Garden Design*, which offered advice on design, hard landscaping and planting, as well as promoting the garden as 'a place for entertaining, for household use … Plants are important, of course, but the first consideration should be the fitness of the garden for family use'.

After he moved to Sussex in 1980, Brookes's client base changed from being urban to those with rural gardens or country estates. The increase in his country-house commissions was also influenced by the publication of his book *A Place in the Country* (1984) that promoted 'the garden ideal of our time: in touch with local ways, local habitats and the creative preservation of the countryside'.

Brookes had long been committed to an environmental agenda and his concern with vernacular gardens and regional diversity was in tune with late 20th century thinking. From the 1970s, an ecological approach to landscape design and planting had found favour with many practitioners, but the desire for more environmentally friendly and less labour-intensive methods of gardening was also reflected in books for amateur gardeners. William Robinson's book *The Wild Garden* (1870) was reprinted in 1977 and 1983 for a new audience looking for informal planting, subdued colours and delicate flowers. Marjorie Fish at East Lambrook Manor in Somerset, Beth Chatto at her Essex home and Joyce Robinson, Brookes's predecessor at Denmans Gardens, West Sussex, were already gardening in this way, creating unusual planting combinations using native and exotic plants. Chatto catalogued the development of her Essex garden and her principles of ecological gardening in her books, such as *The Dry Garden* (1980), *The Damp Garden* (1982) and *Green Tapestry* (1989). Her Gravel Garden on the site of an earlier car park was laid out in 1991–92 and planted with species that required no watering.

RIGHT *Room Outside: A New Approach to Garden Design* by John Brookes, published by Thames & Hudson in 1969

Room Outside a new approach to garden design by JOHN BROOKES

Mid-century designers, such as Percy Cane, Russell Page and Lanning Roper, continued to create more traditional or flower-dominated gardens. Cane's work at Dartington Hall for the Elmhirsts, following work there by Avray Tipping and the American Beatrix Farrand, survives. Page's French inspired gardens were mainly for overseas clients, but his autobiography, *The Education of a Gardener* (1962), documents his career. The American Lanning Roper was inspired by Fish's wild plantings and with his wife, the artist Primrose Harley, developed their Chelsea home as a country cottage garden. Rosemary Verey and Penelope Hobhouse, influenced by Chatto, became celebrated for their decorative plantsmanship. Verey's country-house garden at Barnsley House (Gloucestershire) is a combination of the formal and informal with follies to create focal points. Hobhouse, as the National Trust tenant of 17th century Tintinhull House (Somerset) from 1980–93, restored some of the earlier structure with yew hedges, planting the resultant rooms with striking planting combinations.

From the 1970s three Dutch plantsmen, Ton ter Linden, Henk Gerritson and Piet Oudolf, changed the look of Dutch, British and American gardens with the 'Dutch Wave' or New Perennials Movement. Their naturalistic designs use perennial flowers, such as *Eupatorium* and *Achillea* species, and grasses, such as *Miscanthus* and *Calamagrostis*, that are particularly attractive in late summer and

autumn and whose seed heads will stand in the garden during winter.

A similar exploration of new planting styles was taking place in the United States between landscape architects James van Sweden and Wolfgang Oehme. Termed 'the New American Garden', their plantings incorporate large swathes of grasses and ecologically compatible perennials, creating gardens that 'move in the breeze and sparkle like stained glass'.

These new planting styles have been influential in the UK, notably in the work of Dan Pearson and Tom Stuart-Smith. Since the 1980s, Pearson has studied plants growing in the wild and interpreted this ecological understanding in his designs, emphasising that the natural appearance of the garden is as important as the organic methods used to cultivate it. He describes his own gardens at Home Farm (Northamptonshire) as moving 'from wilderness to wilderness' with a woodland area and a pond blending into sophisticated planting near the house. Stuart-Smith's designs combine 'naturalism and modernity', the meadows, prairies and courtyard of his own garden, The Barn Garden (Hertfordshire), show his design and planting philosophy.

Over the 20th century the focus has moved from plant-centred private gardens to 'gardens for people', but increasing post-war environmental awareness has also changed the way people garden. Since the end of the century, design and planting were influenced by concerns for sustainability and biodiversity, more people belong to environmental organisations and more are prepared to take consumer decisions based on ecological concerns. In 2001 Richard Carew Pole, former president of the Royal Horticultural Society, predicted that 'Garden designers will need to adapt to plant and environmental changes.' In 2002 the report *Gardening in a Global Greenhouse* stated that 'the gardening community has the potential to set an example of good practice... which could ultimately alter the course of climate change'. This is the direction the 20th century private garden is taking into the 21st century.

Barbara Simms

LEFT Hestercombe, Somerset, designed by Gertrude Jekyll

Portmeirion

Location: Near Porthmadog, Portmeirion, Gwynedd
Designed by: Clough Williams-Ellis
Created: 1925–75

Portmeirion is celebrated as a resort village, but it is also the subtlest of designed landscapes. Clough Williams-Ellis found a site of fabulous beauty near his family's home on the Dwyryd estuary where old quays fed his fancy for sailing vessels and mermaids. Here in the 1850s H.S. Westmacott built the house Aber Ia, inspiring Clough's hotel, and planted exotic trees in the Gwyllt wood; so did later owner Caton Haigh while Clough created a theatrical variant of Italy's Portofino. A crag above the sea became a citadel cluster; the combe behind, a theatre where ornamental structures developed over 40 years, with greens and steps radiating from a former walled garden. Clough surrounded his piazza with contrivances of architectural salvage into the 1960s. His play between the scenic and the practical – archways to reveal a view, walls to deny one, sculptures to amuse – is intensified by Himalayan exotics flourishing in the mild microclimate.

Richard Haslam

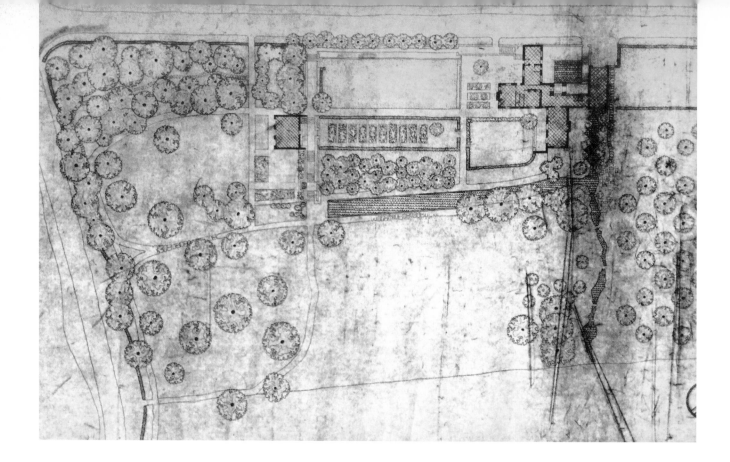

Kingcombe

Location: Chipping Campden,
Gloucestershire
Designed by: Gordon Russell,
Geoffrey Jellicoe and Russell Page
Created: 1926
Registered: Grade II*

In 1926, the designer Gordon Russell moved into his newly completed house, Kingcombe, and set about creating a new garden. Working with Geoffrey Jellicoe and Russell Page through the 1930s, Russell designed a garden that made the most of its situation, with terraces created along the steeply falling ground, allowing a series of 'rooms' at several heights to be enclosed by walls and hedging, offering a variety of inviting and intimate spaces, and wide views over the countryside beyond. The design was unified by Jellicoe's Italian Steps that provided a visual stop to the terraces, enlivened by water running in troughs alongside.

Russell continued to develop the site throughout his life; the result is a garden full of features showing the influence of his designer's eye, and redolent of his character, typified by the playful water conduit in the shape of his own bespectacled portrait head, from which his grandchildren were sent to collect water for the table.

Amanda Hooper

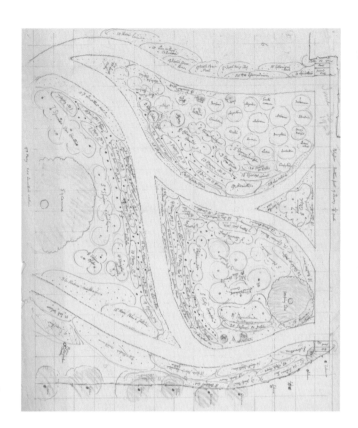

Blagdon Hall

Location: Seaton Burn, Northumberland
Designed by: Gertrude Jekyll and Sir Edwin Lutyens
Created: 1926
Registered: Grade II

Jekyll and Lutyens designed the gardens at Blagdon Hall as an overlay to the 18th and 19th century pleasure grounds. The commission was for Lutyens's daughter, Ursula, who married the 3rd Viscount Ridley in 1924. Lutyens's simple, stately design was implemented in phases between 1926 and 1938 and included a long, staggered canal terminating in a circular pool, a lime avenue, and a walk. Jekyll, ('Aunt Bumps' to Ursula), was in her eighties and nearly blind when she made the designs in 1928–29.

The quarry garden was laid out as a sheltered retreat from cold winds, with branching paths leading through dense planting of flowering shrubs, and perennials such as peonies and iris among larger trees. Her other scheme was herbaceous planting in eight interlinking hexagonal enclosures. This was a living masterwork in colour theory, each section taking the visitor through a progressively stronger palette, with warm tones to combat the northern skies. Jekyll's planting only survives in part but Lutyens's work is largely intact.

Camilla Beresford

Coleton Fishacre

Location: near Kingswear, Devon
Designed by: Oswald Milne and
Edward White of Milner, White & Son
Created: 1926
Registered: Grade II*

Theatre and hotel manager Rupert D'Oyly Carte built a new house in a late Arts and Crafts style on a site dropping down to Pudcombe Cove. The house was designed by Oswald Milne, who probably also collaborated with Lady Dorothy D'Oyly Carte on the garden design. Edward White gave advice on the planting of shelter belts of pines, cypresses, sycamore, evergreen oaks, sea buckthorn and tamarisk.

Visitors descend through a series of spaces that become more enclosed by planting and less formal until reaching the final view of the open sea, framed by a simple stone aedicule. The Rill Garden, with its stone channel and basin enclosed by rough stone walls, is suggestive of Milne's master, Edwin Lutyens. Despite low rainfall, there is continuous underground moisture that encourages the growth of rare plants, including tree ferns, in the sheltered valley. The property passed to the National Trust in 1982, and was opened in 1999.

Alan Powers

Great Yarmouth Venetian Waterways

Location: North Denes, Great Yarmouth, Norfolk
Designed by: S.P. Thompson
Created: 1928, restored 2018–19
Registered: Grade II

Land reclaimed by construction of a new sea wall in Great Yarmouth was used for a boating lake in 1926 and the more sinuous Venetian Waterways two years later. Funded by the council, these projects extended tourist attractions north of the resort centre while providing relief work for some 292 unemployed men over the winter of 1927–28.

The borough surveyor's designs were Venetian only in so far as they resembled a network of canals criss-crossed by bridges. Around the concrete lined channels, imported soil was planted up with drifts of perennials and annuals. Rockeries were another key feature that marked the scheme out as a bold move away from traditional seaside bedding displays. A series of thatched shelters was built among the islands, and visitors could ride in electric boats named after Broadland rivers.

Much of the original planting was lawned over in the 1980s but in May 2019 the waterways re-opened following a £1.7 million lottery-funded restoration.

Kathryn Ferry

Bekonscot
Model Village

Location: Beaconsfield,
Buckinghamshire
Designed by: Roland Callingham
Created: 1929

'Either your model railway goes into the garden, or you do' Mrs Callingham ordered her secretly pleased husband Roland. So household staff transformed the swimming pool into a miniature-islanded sea; rockeries became 'the Swiss garden'; rose borders became fields. By 1929 houseguests were pleading for them to open to the public – so they did.

The ensuing 'Bekonscot' was not the first model village, but it is the most influential. It spawned hundreds of imitators worldwide and inspired countless young wannabe-architects.

Today, it has received over 15 million visitors and makes a fortune for charity. Its 0.75 acres (0.3ha) of surprisingly recent buildings are more considered than the naïve stone-and-timber cottages rambling across the original garden landscape, but it still delights and entertains. Stomping around like Gulliver in Lilliput, we see why it remains the best – and the most fun – of all model villages. Roland would be pleased.

Tim Dunn

1930–
1949

Sissinghurst Castle

Location: Near Cranbrook, Kent
Designed by: Vita Sackville-West and Harold Nicolson
Created: 1930
Registered: Grade I

In 1930, poet and writer Vita Sackville-West and her husband, author and diplomat Harold Nicolson, bought 16th-century Sissinghurst Castle, a dilapidated tower and outhouses set in 450 acres in the Weald of Kent. They restored Priests House and South Cottage as living accommodation and the tower as Sackville-West's private sanctuary and writing room. A five-acre garden of rooms, including the Rondel, Rose and Spring Gardens, was developed from 'a complete wilderness'; the now-celebrated White Garden was created after 1945. Sackville-West was a skilled and knowledgeable plantswoman while Nicolson designed the layout, creating between them a garden of 'profusion, even extravagance and exuberance, within the confines of the utmost linear severity' (Sackville-West, 1942).

They continued developing the garden until Sackville-West's death from cancer at Sissinghurst in 1962; Nicolson died six years later. Garden-making at Sissinghurst inspired Sackville-West's writings, including the poems *Sissinghurst* and *The Garden*. The estate was gifted to the National Trust in 1967.

Barbara Simms

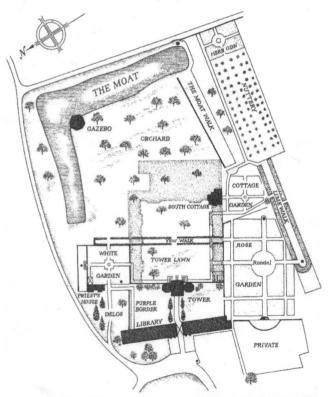

THE GARDEN OF
SISSINGHURST
·CASTLE·

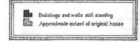

Buildings and walls still standing
Approximate extent of original house

Langdon Plotlands

Location: Langdon, Essex
Designed by: Residents
Created: 1930

Essex plotlands originated in the late Victorian agricultural crisis, enabling farmers to unload worthless land. The plots attracted a flood of east London families between the wars who planted fruit trees, kept bees and grew vegetables, while camping in rudimentary shelters. During World War II, these shacks became home to many who had been bombed out of their homes and jobs, often in the docks. Orchards and productive gardens took shape along the unmetalled tracks.

The settlers paid no rates, as they had no amenities, but were targeted for compulsory purchase to build Basildon. Today in Langdon, The Haven is the plotlands museum, giving a sense of the old landscape, while in South Woodham Ferrers, a community orchard commemorates the plotlands there. These ad hoc landscapes were a testament to self-determination in the face of considerable hardship, and a reminder of a less regulated society, often with rural roots only a generation or two away.

Gillian Darley

Tintinhill House

Location: Yeovil, Somerset
Designed by: Phyllis Reiss
and Penelope Hobhouse
Created: 1933
Registered: Grade II

Penelope Hobhouse described Tintinhull as 'A Hidcote in miniature; two acres instead of ten'. Captain and Mrs Reiss bought the 17th-century house in 1933 and created a series of garden rooms, as at Hidcote, enclosed by clipped yew with abundant planting designed to give colour and texture throughout the year.

The asymmetrical sequence of six main rooms gives axial views that make the garden seem larger, an effect enhanced by changes of scale, as between the Fountain Garden – almost filled by a round pool with white plants in the spandrels – and the specimen tree set in the generous lawn and borders of the Cedar Court. Planting is decisive: massed catmint in the kitchen garden, a bed just of bearded irises, big stone pots of lilies.

Mrs Reiss donated the property to the National Trust before her death in 1961 and, having become its tenant in 1980, Hobhouse developed the garden in her spirit.

Susannah Charlton

Stoke Poges Gardens of Remembrance

Location: Stoke Poges, Buckinghamshire
Designed by: Edward White
Created: 1935–37
Registered: Grade I

Designer Edward White (1872–1952), director of Milner, White & Son and president of the Landscape Institute, was involved in the contemporary cremation movement, including lecturing and publishing for the Cremation Society.

The gardens were laid out on land that formed part of Stoke Park, adjoining St. Giles' Church of Gray's *Elegy Written in a Country Churchyard*. Their design was pioneering as non-denominational memorial gardens for the repose of cremated ashes, without 'buildings, erections or monuments of any kind likely to remind one of a cemetery'.

The site is designed on a grand scale across 20 acres (8ha) as a complete garden with characteristic period features including a formal Italianate sunken garden, colonnade with pergola, rock and water garden, rose garden, parterres, basins, ponds, rills and fountains, all set against an informality of shrubbery, woodland and parkland lawns. Within this structure were 500 gated and hedged, individually designed, paved family plots, and 3,000 individual plots.

Marylla Hunt

Dolphin Square

Location: Pimlico, London
Designed by: Richard Sudell
Created: 1935
Registered: Grade II

The private inter-war housing development at Dolphin Square contains rare surviving gardens designed by the celebrated pioneer landscape architect Richard Sudell. An oasis in busy Westminster, the design works with the architecture using the projecting wings of the flats to create different garden experiences. Each of these discrete and secluded spaces was planted by Sudell to reflect the atmosphere of a different country, with native plants chosen to thrive in the particular microclimate of each recess. The open square features a more formal layout of lawns, a central avenue of horse chestnuts, rose garden and (originally) a fountain.

Sadly, the Spanish and Mexican Garden, located by Sudell on the roof of the amenity building to maximise exposure to the sun, was lost in a reconfiguration in the 1990s. Despite its addition to Historic England's Register, parts of the remaining garden are threatened by development proposals for additional hotel space.

Clare Price

Derry and Toms Roof Garden

Location: Kensington High Street, Kensington, London
Designed by: Ralph Hancock
Created: 1936-38
Registered: Grade II

This spectacular roof garden was designed for Derry and Toms department store, for their customers. It was the largest of its type in the world, but had parallels in New York where Hancock designed the Rockefeller Center roof gardens.

The 1.48 acre (6000m) sixth floor garden has a complex design, laid out in three distinct areas. The exotic Spanish Garden is complete with a Moorish folly and pergola, canal and fountain, and takes in the view of St Mary Abbots's spire. The south-facing Sun Pavilion opens onto the central informal woodland garden that supports surprisingly large trees and featured exotic planting arranged around an informal stream, pools, bridges and even eye-catching flamingos.

Lunettes in the enclosing wall afford long views south over London. The intimate Tudor-style English Garden is defined by red brick walls, stone arches and Old English scented plants and climbers. The garden has been used as an exclusive entertainment venue but closed in 2018.

Sarah Rutherford and Sarah Couch

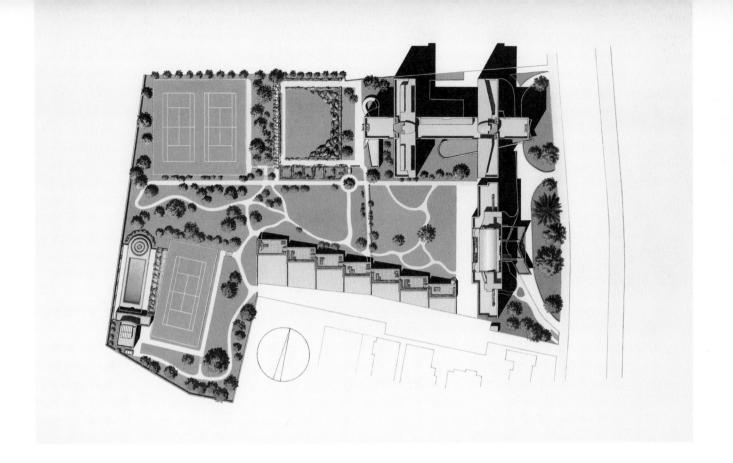

The Gardens at Highpoint

Location: North Hill, Highgate, Greater London
Designed by: Berthold Lubetkin and Tecton, with Clarence Elliott (plantsman)
Created: 1935 and 1938

The international renown of Highpoint has tended to focus on the architecture, distracting attention from the totality of Lubetkin's composition of buildings and site, that together represent the most complete realisation of a particular urban planning model – compact apartments in a recreational landscape offering an idealised vision of modern living. Just as the two blocks complement each other – Highpoint I a sculpture, Highpoint II an assembly, so do the earlier and later gardens – the first a geometric abstraction, the second a contrived caprice of winding paths and arabesque lawns – the two halves being bound together by the armature of the central walkway. The garage roofs may no longer be used as a raised promenade but their echelon form still provides the perfect architectural attenuation leading to the grand finale of tennis courts and swimming pool. And Lubetkin's inspiration for this lesson in modern classicism? Kenwood House half a mile down the road.

John Allan

St Ann's Court

Location: Egham, Surrey
Designed by: Christopher Tunnard
Created: 1938
Registered: Grade II*

In *Gardens in the Modern Landscape* (1938), Canadian-born Christopher Tunnard (1910–79) claimed 'it is the duty of the landscape architect, as well as the architect, to adapt and use [concrete, steel and glass] in harmonious compositions.' At St Ann's Court (originally St Ann's Hill), he collaborated with the Australian-born architect Raymond McGrath who replaced an earlier dwelling with a spectacular concrete drum-shaped hilltop house (itself Grade II*).

Tunnard edited mature existing planting and restored a late Georgian grotto and tea house. The 'modern' part of the garden is a terrace extending from the south side of the house where a glazed temperate house is set back behind a small pool, terminated by a curved wall, adapted from existing fabric. A Paul Nash-like concrete beam with two openings frames the view and blurs the inside/outside distinction, while a Willi Soukop abstract sculpture originally terminated the view. Below the house towards the north, a curved swimming pool echoes the drum shape.

Alan Powers

Hope Cement Works

Location: Castleton, Derbyshire
Designed by: Geoffrey Jellicoe
and Sheila Haywood
Created: 1943

Hope Cement Works (now Breedon Group) sits at the heart of the Peak District National Park. Designed for the quarry site in 1943, it was Jellicoe's first such masterplan and has stood the test of time, despite the increased area devoted to quarrying on the site, well beyond anything predicted. At Jellicoe's death in 1996 it remained a contained, coherent, industrial scene embedded within one of the finest stretches of upland landscape in the country, a modern variant on the Sublime. Jellicoe's decision to respect, even aggrandise, the strongly marked valley and hill landscape gave it staying power. He kept the line of the escarpment inviolate, while allowing the quarrying and the accommodation of waste to seep out in a south-westerly direction. Around it all, heavy tree planting has paid dividends in landscape terms. Above all, the site owners remained faithful to Jellicoe's radically simple, but bold, designed landscape.

Gillian Darley

Great Dixter

Location: Northiam, East Sussex
Designed by: Sir Edwin Lutyens, planting by George Thorold and Nathaniel and Daisy Lloyd, planting redesigned by Christopher Lloyd
Created: 1912, gardened by Christopher Lloyd from 1948
Registered: Grade I

Great Dixter was the home of Christopher Lloyd (1921–2006), who used it to showcase his planting ideas and inspire his informed and witty writing. Lloyd's original plant and colour combinations continue to inspire readers and gardeners. When Lloyd's father Nathaniel retired from his printing business to become an amateur architect and photographer, he commissioned Edwin Lutyens as the architect for the house and garden. Lutyens designed a series of linked garden compartments around the existing medieval and 18th-century buildings. George Thorold provided the early planting scheme, Nathaniel Lloyd bought yews to shape into topiary, and Daisy Lloyd sowed wildflower meadows. The preservation of the early 20th-century structure provides the backdrop and foil for the striking and continually changing planting displays. Christopher Lloyd's head gardener Fergus Garrett has continued the innovative gardening traditions at Great Dixter that is now a charitable trust.

Camilla Beresford

Barbara Hepworth Sculpture Garden

Location: St Ives, Cornwall
Designed by: Barbara Hepworth
Created: 1949
Registered: Grade II

Sculptors and artists Barbara Hepworth and her husband Ben Nicholson came to live in Carbis Bay, Cornwall with their young family at the outbreak of war in 1939. Finding inspiration in the dramatic landscape, Hepworth bought Trewyn Studio in 1949 (now the Barbara Hepworth Museum and Sculpture Garden) in nearby St Ives. The garden allowed her both to work in the open air and to display her collection of abstract stone and bronze sculptures, largely influenced by nature. She designed the garden (possibly assisted by composer Ivy Priaulx Rainier) with views and vistas using architectural plants, ferns, bamboos and ornamental trees as settings for her sculptures. Most of the sculptures remain as she placed them, including the six-part bronze sculpture, *Conversation with Magic Stones* (1973).

Following Hepworth's wishes, Trewyn Studio and much of her work was given to the nation after her death in 1975, and placed in the care of the Tate Gallery in 1980.

Barbara Simms

1950–1959

Mark Hall North

Location: Off First Avenue, Harlow,
Essex
Designed by: Frederick Gibberd and
Sylvia Crowe
Created: 1950–54

Gibberd defined his new town at Harlow using landscape, identifying the valley
bottoms and stream beds as the most interesting elements of the rolling Essex
countryside. These wedges of open land divided the housing neighbourhoods into
four main groups.

The first housing was laid out in parkland at Mark Hall, a country house
destroyed by fire in 1947. Gibberd retained the setting of St Mary's Church
and nearby brook as open land, the old lane becoming a cycle path and Henry
Moore's *Family Group* sited near the children's playground (now moved; instead
Antanas Brazdy's *Solo Flight* dominates the vista). Existing mature specimen trees
and higher wooded land determined the layout of two curving drives of housing.
Smaller roads were angled on clumps of trees, the church tower or a new
eyecatcher – Britain's first point block, The Lawns, a means of retaining a group
of oak trees and creating a contrast in scale.

Elain Harwood

Festival Pleasure Gardens

Location: Battersea, London
Designed by: James Gardner
Created: 1951

The Battersea Pleasure Gardens opened in May 1951 as part of the Festival of Britain. Designed to sit on 37 acres (15 ha) requisitioned from Thames-side Battersea Park, the gardens gave relief and relaxation to festival visitors weary after touring the South Bank Exhibition further downstream. Chief designer was James Gardner, working with the architects Harrison & Seel. The gardens recalled the former glory of the long-since disappeared pleasure gardens of Vauxhall (an inspiration for the designers) and offered a grotto, miniature railway, theatres, walk, Mississippi Show Boat and huge tented dance pavilion. Osbert Lancaster's Fountain Lake was brought alive at night by decorative lighting, while John Piper's Grand Vista had fantastical Gothic structures made of cane-work. By popular demand, the funfair stayed open until 1974 and in 2002 remains of the Festival Gardens reopened following extensive restoration.

Harriet Atkinson

Alton East and Alton West Estates

Location: Roehampton, London
Designed by: London County Council Architect's Department
Created: Alton East 1952–56, Alton West 1954–61

The Alton estates fuse Modern Movement architecture with the British love of landscape and the picturesque. Alton East is on a wooded, steeply sloping site, with over 700 mature trees, including a fine mulberry, alongside shrubberies and lawns. Dilapidated and war-damaged Victorian villas were demolished and point blocks and maisonettes built in their gardens, with outstanding views over Roehampton and Wimbledon Common.

Alton West is set in a grander landscape of rolling parkland, part by Capability Brown, the perfect foil to its more formal architecture of squarish point blocks, boxy maisonettes, and five slab blocks, stepping dramatically up the hill on their pilotis. A grassy valley dotted with three 18th-century villas contains mature trees including an avenue of poplars and limes and a magnificent Lebanon cedar. As a child I remember a ha-ha separating where I lived at Alton West from a golf course, but have never found any proof of this.

Suzanne Waters

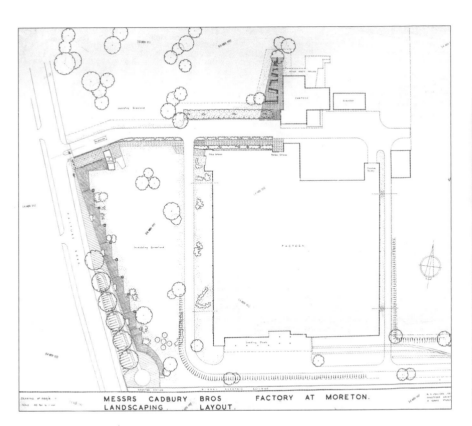

MESSRS CADBURY BROS FACTORY AT MORETON.
LANDSCAPING. LAYOUT.

Cadbury Factory

Location: Moreton, Merseyside
Designed by: Geoffrey Jellicoe
Created: 1952–54

When Cadbury's decided that chocolate biscuit production was more appropriately located in the cooler and windier climate of the Wirral peninsula, Jellicoe was appointed to design the new factory garden and sports fields. He found it a 'diabolical' site, 'dull, severe and intensely primitive', imagining it a million years before 'infested with vast prehistoric monsters'. He proposed bunds in the shape of extended serpents, wide shelterbelts and tree planting.

But Jellicoe's most inventive and delightful part of this project is his modernist design of the concrete lined canal along the street boundary leading to the station. Weirs divided it into ten pools (now nine) each shaped to exaggerate the perspective and with its own raised planting bed. There are viewing platforms suspended over the water.

It was the experimental ground and precursor for Jellicoe's design for the Water Gardens at Hemel Hempstead, partly repeated at Shute and elsewhere.

Annabel Downs

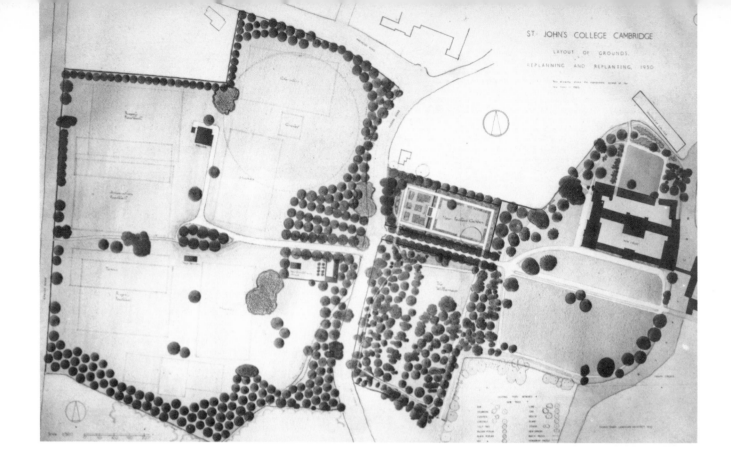

Scholars' Garden, St John's College

Location: Cambridge, Cambridgeshire
Designed by: Thomas Wilfred Sharp and Sylvia Crowe
Created: 1952

In 1949–51, St John's College commissioned Sharp and Crowe to propose a planting strategy in response to a decaying tree population. The work included the design of a new Scholars' Garden in a former orchard, implemented in 1952. Although little-known now, Sharp was a central figure in mid-20th century planning and the author of a number of influential and popular books. His work at St John's College is a rare surviving example of his landscape design. He planned the hard landscaping and designed a shelter in 1954 in conjunction with David Wyn Roberts (1911–82), then teaching at the Cambridge University School of Architecture. Crowe, one of the pre-eminent and pioneering mid-20th century British landscape designers, supervised the contract for St John's and designed the planting scheme for the garden of roses, rosemary, peonies, and other woody shrubs interspersed with Japanese anemones and lilies. Although much of the planting has been lost, the structure, paths and pavilion are intact.

Camilla Beresford

Golden Lane Estate

Location: City of London
Designed by: Chamberlin, Powell & Bon
Created: 1952–63

In 1951–52 the City Corporation held a competition to design flats for key workers. Joe Chamberlin, Geoffry Powell and Christoph Bon submitted an entry each, and formed a partnership when Powell won. His scheme of low blocks surrounding a central tower was arranged around courtyards that turned their backs on the blitzed neighbourhood.

As built, the tower became taller. Powell exploited the deep basements left by warehousing previously on the site to sink the simple, grassed courtyards, one with a pool. A central circular bastion, a historicist feature, contrasts sharply with the curtain-walled housing. Chamberlin designed a roof garden on top of the tower, featuring a pool and pergola, while extensions from 1954 and 1957– 63 included tennis courts and a paved area over car parking. Powell declared that 'there is no attempt at the informal in these courts... We have no desire to make the project look like a garden suburb'.

Elain Harwood

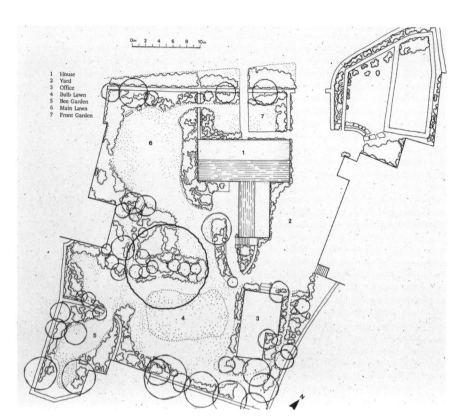

1 House
2 Yard
3 Office
4 Bulb Lawn
5 Bee Garden
6 Main Lawn
7 Front Garden

Little Peacocks Garden

Location: Filkins, Oxfordshire
Designed by: Brenda Colvin
Created: 1954

After her presidency of the Institute of Landscape Architects (1951–53) as the first woman president of any of the environmental or engineering professions, Brenda Colvin (1887–1981) purchased Little Peacocks, a Cotswold house near Lechlade, in 1954. It was not until 1965 that she moved her office from London to live and practice in Filkins, from 1969 in partnership with Hal Moggridge. However she immediately started to create the half-acre (0.2ha) garden, most of which had previously been a farmyard, enclosed and partitioned by stone walls. The garden contains a large collection of her favourite plants, so arranged that it reads as a flowing spatial composition of sunny lawn contrasted with deep shade below a horse chestnut, all enriched by her sensibility to the texture and colour of plants. The garden has been conserved by the practice that continues at Little Peacocks, as Colvin had hoped.

Hal Moggridge

GEOFFREY JELLICOE
AND THE LANDSCAPE PROFESSION

Is it possible to tell the story of British 20th-century landscape and gardens through one individual? If so, that person would have to be Sir Geoffrey Jellicoe (1900–96), not only for his long life and career, but for his role in the history of ideas and the redefinition of the boundary lines of professional practice. Architect, planner, landscape and garden designer, writer and philosopher and professional leader, perhaps the only absence from the list is plantsman – something for which Jellicoe relied on his wife Susan, herself a significant writer on gardens. Academic Tom Turner claimed in the journal *Landscape* 'Jellicoe … brought intellectual, artistic and institutional clarity to what remains an ill-defined professional activity of uncertain parentage'.

Jellicoe studied at the Architectural Association (AA) in London, where the dominant style in the early 1920s was classical. With a fellow student, J.C. (Jock) Shepherd, he toured Italy on a travel scholarship to survey and draw up the plans and levels of major Renaissance gardens, resulting in a publication in 1925 that has remained a classic, and planted the seed of Jellicoe's interest in the combination of architecture and gardening. During the 1920s, he combined practice with teaching at the AA, and discovered modern art, writing one of the first reviews of sculpture by Henry Moore. Early in 1928, Jellicoe contributed a garden scheme for the modernist 'House of the Future' at the Ideal Home Exhibition in a French Art Deco manner.

In architecture and gardens alike, there was in around 1930 a turn to Georgian formality (different to the Edwardian classicism of Harold Peto or Thomas Mawson) and also to modernism. Jellicoe's Caveman Restaurant, Cheddar Gorge, of 1934–36 was included in the New York exhibition 'Modern Architecture in England' three years later. A shallow pool with a glass block base in the terrace that formed the roof allowed the diners below to see goldfish moving overhead. But Jellicoe could play the other card, creating an unrestrained Baroque parterre water garden for Ronald and Nancy Tree, complementing the mid-18th century Ditchley Park in 1936 – a different kind of playfulness. Landscape and garden design did not demand the same style policing as architecture, a discovery also made by his younger contemporary, Christopher Tunnard, whose book, *Gardens in the Modern Landscape*, 1938, was open-ended and pluralist in its interpretation of 'modern'. As Tim Richardson has written, 'it was not anathema to Jellicoe, or to other modernists such as Crowe or Colvin, to work in a historical context: in fact, 18th-century landscape parks were a major influence. Jellicoe described his approach at St. Paul's Walden Bury, Hertfordshire, in which he imaginatively recreated glades, statue groups and other formal features, as "neo-historicist"', comparing this reworking to Ezra Pound's doctrine of 'creative translation' of Chinese or Anglo-Saxon poetry.

RIGHT House of the Future, garden by Geoffrey Jellicoe, illustrated by Walpole Champneys

The architect Thomas Mawson (1861–1933) set a precedent in Britain for combining garden design, landscape and town planning into one hybrid practice. The terms 'landscape designer' and 'landscape architect' were first adopted in the United States and the planner Thomas Adams suggested that an Institute of Landscape Architects was more appropriate than a proposed British Association of Garden Architects. Later renamed as the Landscape Institute, it was founded in 1929 with Jellicoe amongst its first members. This was the beginning of an endless struggle for recognition as a distinct practice. Many early members had an architecture background, but it was two women whose design careers stemmed from a horticultural training, Brenda Colvin and Sylvia Crowe, who in 1945 spoke out effectively against assimilation of the ILA with the RIBA. The intellectual and spiritual guide for the profession, however, was arguably Patrick Geddes (1854–1932), especially in his disdain for demarcations between different sectors of knowledge and his combination of visionary ambition with the ability to implement small-scale demonstration projects.

Skilful wartime manoeuvres, with Jellicoe as president of the ILA in 1939–49, helped to ensure that landscape architects were employed as consultants for many new projects for the welfare state's planned redemption of the scarred landscape of extractive industry and uncontrolled development. The public mood was increasingly in favour of such controls and a new interpretive script was composed, typified by Nikolaus Pevsner's *The Englishness of English Art* (1955, originally Reith Lectures on the Home Service), whose closing chapter celebrated the landscape setting of the LCC's Alton estates as a continuation of the national genius for the picturesque, while in the same year, Ian Nairn's *Outrage* castigated the failure to live up to such ideals. Landscape practitioners contributed major texts, such as Colvin's *Land and Landscape* (1947), at once poetic and practical, and Crowe's *Tomorrow's Landscape* (1956), followed by her studies of the landscape treatment of roads and electric power installations. This was arguably the landscape profession's moment of greatest hope.

Colvin and Crowe both became important post-war practitioners, engaged on new towns, university campuses and power stations. Jellicoe played a role in each case, in 1948 producing a masterplan for Hemel Hempstead, although a second plan for the town centre was rejected. He returned in 1959 to lay out the Water Gardens, where we see his symbolic approach, based on subconscious archetypes, beginning to appear. He designed a university campus at Nottingham, imperfectly realised by others, and a 'Landscape of Power' at Oldbury-on-Severn. His architectural practice during this period (with Allan Ballantyne and F.S. Coleridge), included the Civic Centre at Plymouth, a large-scale tower and podium, integrated through paving and pools with the pedestrian axis running through the rebuilt city. It remains opaque how much he personally contributed to the actual architecture of the firm's projects, as opposed to their landscape elements. He formally closed the office in 1973, well past normal retirement age, and worked with Susan Jellicoe on a comprehensive pictorial history, *The Landscape of Man* (1975). This book did much to bridge the localised geographical study of landscape to wider themes of cultural progress, although his prediction that 'the world is moving into a phase when landscape design may well be recognized as the most comprehensive of the arts' has largely remained unfulfilled, as has an ecological age, the first false-dawn of which he optimistically anticipated in his conclusion.

A decade earlier, Jellicoe's commission in late 1963 to create the memorial to J.F. Kennedy at Runnymede represented a conceptual breakthrough. He was happy to reveal the narrative behind it, based on Bunyan's *Pilgrim's Progress*, but its modesty as a monument and planting scheme arising from this allegory, allied to the deployment of the contours and views to create an experience of asymmetrical movement, created a new synthesis of implicit and explicit meanings. This self-interpretation preceded the beginning of the deeper iconographic study of familiar 18th-century gardens, exemplified by Kenneth

Woodbridge's study of Stourhead, *Landscape and Antiquity* (1970) that unearthed the personal and mythological dimensions of Henry Hoare's re-telling of Virgil's *Aeneid*. Jellicoe was convinced of C.J. Jung's theory of the collective unconscious, through which the classical references of his earlier work could be seen as symbolic in a new light.

There followed a series of late commissions for Jellicoe that, although private and not easily accessible, were widely published. The most important were the remodelling of the gardens at Shute (1969–93) for Michael Tree, the son of his pre-war patron, and his wife Anne; and Sutton Place (1980–83) for the American Stanley Seeger. While different in character, each offered Jellicoe a new scope to develop his Jungian ideas about the duality of human nature through a range of references to art and landscape, including an enlarged version of a Ben Nicholson white relief from the 1930s reflected in a pool at Sutton Place. These commissions, and some extravagant but unexecuted projects in Modena, Texas and Atlanta, Georgia, helped Jellicoe achieve an unprecedented celebrity in the last years of his life, with books, a return to teaching at Thames Polytechnic and a television programme.

There have been a number of other architects who practised equally as landscape and garden designers, such as Peter Shepheard, Ivor Cunningham (working mainly with Eric Lyons) and Peter Aldington, but more formal

RIGHT Ditchley Park, Oxfordshire

training courses since the 1960s have tended to firmly separate the professions. Architects Patel Taylor were successful in their competition wins with the French garden designer Allain Provost, first at Thames Barrier Park and then Eastside Park in Birmingham, since France, as in the 17th century, became again the source of disciplined style for England. 'Landscape Urbanism', a hybrid practice first named in Australia and developed in the United States, would not, one suspects, have appealed to Jellicoe, since it is often insensitive to local character and arbitrary in its imposition of form. Perhaps Jellicoe's more wacky projects for the Pilkington's 'Glass Age' promotional series, such as 'Motopia' (a road on top of buildings) or filling Soho with canals, might qualify as Landscape Urbanism in terms of their attention-grabbing extravagance.

How effective the 'Jellicoe boom' of the 1990s was in securing the long-term place of landscape in design culture and popular understanding may be questioned. If it failed, this would be because funding for the public realm has become less dependable, owing to political swings and the self-punishing decade of austerity. Activity has tended to take the form of eye-catching projects (from garden festivals to 'fun' urban face-lifting) rather than the steady joining up of parts to form cohesive wholes and ensure their long-term maintenance. The considerable achievement represented, for example, by Mile End Park in Tower Hamlets, both in its patient fulfilment of Patrick Abercrombie's *Greater London Plan* of 1945 and of a 1995 masterplan by Tibbalds Monroe that made subtle adjustments to accommodate the needs of a diverse local population, is not so well known. The 'stars' in this field are now the garden designers who are known from television, rather than landscape architects.

This decline in public profile, if not in quality of work, may be owing to a growing mistrust of professional skills, mirrored in the squeezing out of architectural values. An example is the politically driven shift from the Royal Fine Art Commission, on which a post-war consensus about the nature of the public good in design was maintained, through the often-beneficial activity of its replacement, CABE, to the latter's shrinkage to a much smaller consultancy service.

Soon, however, it may literally be 'closing time in the gardens of the West', as Cyril Connolly wrote in 1949. All predictions about the future of landscapes are now under question from imminent and unstoppable climate change and rising sea levels. Jellicoe and his generation may still inspire us with their steadfast belief in making poetry out of raw nature and bringing their discipline to the centre of public affairs.

Alan Powers

LEFT Sutton Place, Surrey (top); Design for Motopia, Geoffrey Jellicoe (bottom)

Dounreay Experimental Research Establishment

Location: Thurso, Caithness
Designed by: United Kingdom
Atomic Energy Authority
Created: 1954–58

The siting of the government's first fast breeder reactor establishment on Scotland's north coast brought pioneering nuclear technology to a rural landscape. By 1966, Dounreay's steel reactor containment sphere was considered one of the symbols of British science: it represented the antithesis of domineering brick power stations. Coupled with its flat, open coastal location, Dounreay stood out in a new landscape for a new, clean industry. Sylvia Crowe in 1958 considered it a 'cosmic' shape that related to the sky and mountains rather than 'the human scale'. More prosaically, it was a monument to modernity.

As an elemental structure, Dounreay disrupted the landscape. Yet through disruption came celebration, as also seen in the landscaping of the Magnox power stations built across the country between 1956 and 1971. Here the integration of architecture and topography was carefully considered to mutual advantage, preserving visual amenity whilst honouring the place of technology in the landscape.

Linda Ross

Gleadless Valley

Location: Sheffield, South Yorkshire
Designed by: Sheffield City Architect's
Department under J.L. Womersley
Created: 1955–62

A steep-sided valley with a north-facing slope was a difficult place to build housing, and a controversial use of a beauty spot popular with ramblers. But Sheffield was acutely short of land, and Gleadless offered accommodation for 17,000 people in a virtual new town. The valley bottom of the Meers Brook was preserved as Rollestone Wood, with playing fields, while the slightly flatter upper parts were developed in three groups separated by further woodland.

The council produced special plans for housing 'along the contours', with living rooms on the upper levels to exploit the views, contrasted with narrow terraces 'across the contours', their pathways angled to minimise gradients for prams. Best is the view from Blackstock Road, where six-storey flats entered at mid-level (obviating the need for lifts) look across the valley to Donald Martin-Smith's Holy Cross Church, whose soaring roof sweeps high above patio houses set into the hillside.

Elain Harwood

Lollard Street Adventure Playground

Location: Lambeth, London
Designed by: Lady Allen of Hurtwood
Created: 1955

'Better a broken bone than a broken spirit' was a favourite saying of Lady Allen, who was largely responsible for introducing adventure playgrounds to the UK. In 1946 she visited a junk playground in Copenhagen set up under Nazi occupation by the Danish landscape architect Carl Theodor Sørensen. Lady Allen saw that such spaces offered the physical and imaginative freedom children were finding playing in London's bombsites. She wrote an article in *Picture Post* and started a campaign. Lollard Street was one of the first two adventure playgrounds created under the National Playing Fields Association. Not everything worked: a soil mountain proved too messy, but an old lifeboat was a big success. Lady Allen maintained that the two essentials for a successful adventure playground were 'a massive supply of materials and a resourceful and sympathetic leader'. Lollard Street's proximity to Westminster ensured influential visitors and press coverage, and it survives today.

Catherine Croft

Harvey's
Roof Garden

Location: Guildford, Surrey
Designed by: Geoffrey Jellicoe
Created: 1956
Registered: Grade II

Geoffrey Jellicoe completed 60 landscape schemes, some of which had symbolism or allegory as their basis, influenced by the artist Paul Klee's belief that the creative process occurs at a subconscious level.

In 1956 Jellicoe was commissioned to design a roof garden for Harvey's Store (now House of Fraser) above the shopping centre of Guildford. His design for a café and water garden with views to the North Downs was inspired by a Sputnik then circling the earth, and was intended to mimic the first view of earth from space. Jellicoe described it as 'a sky garden' that united heaven and earth. There were seating areas on two levels and a viewing platform on top of the café. Concrete was used for the terrace area, the organic-shaped planting islands and the circular stepping stones across the shallow water. Although neglected from the late 1970s, the café and roof garden were restored in 2000.

Barbara Simms

American Cemetery

Location: Madingley, Cambridge
Designed by: Olmsted Brothers
Created: 1954–56
Registered: Grade I

American cemeteries, since the influential Green-Wood Cemetery in Brooklyn (1938), had long been designed as much for the living as the dead. It was in that tradition that the influential Olmsted Brothers, working with Boston architects Perry Shaw & Hepburn, Kehoe & Dean, designed this World War II cemetery on land gifted by Cambridge University. The headstones are arranged in a vast fan to take advantage of the extensive views north-east towards Ely. Along the southernmost edge of the site, an avenue with three centrally positioned ponds links the flagpole to the chapel. That this is the final resting place of 3,812 American war dead and the site of a memorial to the missing, commemorating 5,127 more, is evoked through an optimistic modernity, rather than the sombre classicism of the British Cemeteries. For that contrast it remains one of the most powerfully uplifting cemetery sites built by the Allies anywhere.

Jon Wright

The Civic Square

Location: Plymouth, Devon
Designed by: Sir Geoffrey Jellicoe
Created: 1957–62
Registered: Grade II

City architect Hector J.W. Stirling originally developed ideas for a 'Great Square' in 1951, as the focus of a civic precinct in the post-war reconstruction of Plymouth, but it was executed by Jellicoe in 1957–62.

Jellicoe planned a pedestrianised square to be enjoyed by Plymouth's townspeople. He created a formal garden around a central L-shaped pond with a circular island, fountains and both soft and hard landscaping, incorporating surviving trees that he encircled with seats. He used a wide variety of materials, including reinforced concrete and Plymouth Limestone, reflecting the facades of the surrounding buildings.

Although suffering from the loss of features such as the post-top lanterns, and the introduction of an unsympathetic modern café, the square still retains much of its original design, including the circular concrete seats and raised biomorphic beds. It has just been designated a Conservation Area, with plans for its refurbishment alongside a remodelled Civic Centre.

Esther Robinson Wild

Gibberd Garden

Location: Marsh Lane, Gilden Way, Harlow, Essex
Designed by: Frederick Gibberd
Created: 1957–84
Registered: Grade II

As early as 1951 Gibberd wrote of wanting a country garden, but his first wife, Thea, loved London. The compromise was a weekend house, and in January 1957 they bought a smallholding just outside Harlow, the new town planned by Gibberd. He added a living room to the house, whose three large windows overlook three contrasting, hedged garden rooms. From a terrace on the north side steps descend to a pool and gazebo, the work of previous owners remodelled by Gibberd. The lower parts of the garden are wilder, where Gibberd dammed the Pincey Brook, created a moated castle and erected columns salvaged from his rebuilding of Coutts Bank in London.

The garden had only three sculptures when in 1972 Gibberd married his second wife, Patricia. She bought him Gerda Rubinstein's *City*, and by 1984 there were over 80 pieces, for which Gibberd created settings using concrete, cobbles, tiles and planting.

Elain Harwood

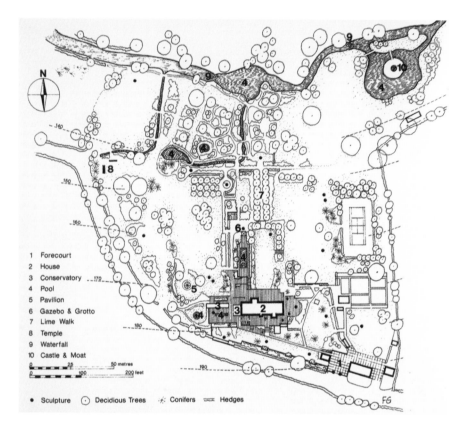

1 Forecourt
2 House
3 Conservatory
4 Pool
5 Pavilion
6 Gazebo & Grotto
7 Lime Walk
8 Temple
9 Waterfall
10 Castle & Moat

0   25   50 metres
0   100   200 feet

• Sculpture   ⊙ Decidious Trees   ✳ Conifers   ⌇ Hedges

F6

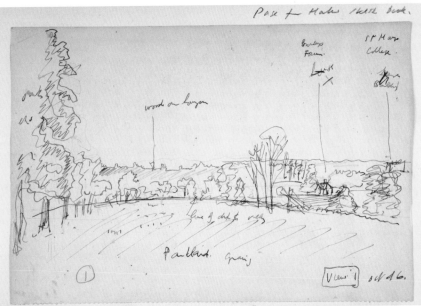

Hemel Hempstead, Water gardens.

Hemel Water Gardens

Location: Hemel Hempstead, Hertfordshire
Designed by: Sir Geoffrey Jellicoe
Created: 1957–59
Registered: Grade II

Hemel Water Gardens were just one element within Jellicoe's 1947 masterplan for the new town of Hemel Hempstead; in the end, they would be his major contribution. Returning to design them in 1957, Jellicoe envisaged the water as something akin to London's Serpentine and it is the keynote in the design of both the gardens and the town centre. By damming the River Gade to the south, he concocted a progression of weirs, bridges and viewing platforms over about 1,000 yards (900m), always framed by the mature trees on site.

The gardens immediately provided an alternative, delightful, spine to the town. The full scheme, along with the planting by Susan Jellicoe, the plantswoman in their partnership (as he always admitted), was upgraded and refreshed with Heritage Lottery funding in 2015–17. This returned the Water Gardens, and the quiet but effective hard landscaping that knits it all together, to centre stage in Hemel Hempstead.

Gillian Darley

Trawsfynydd Power Station

Location: Trawsfynydd, Gwynedd
Designed by: Sir Basil Spence and Dame Sylvia Crowe
Created: 1959–65

Trawsfynydd power station was opened by the Queen on a June day so miserable that even this massive sculptural monolith could barely be seen through the rain.

The challenge had been how to accommodate it in a National Park. Sylvia Crowe had set out her approach in *The Landscape of Power*, published the year before, learning from several recently built power stations. She aimed to achieve 'scale domination' within an open landscape, incorporating an expansive body of water – created in the 1920s to supply water for the Maentwrog hydro-electric power station – and carefully selected tree planting. The collaboration between Crowe and Spence has been likened to that of 18th-century landscape designers with Georgian architects. They intended the main buildings to be seen in the same spirit as a medieval castle. Trawsfynydd was decommissioned in 2009 but is still more sublime as a ruin.

Anthony Blee and Johanna Gibbons

1960–
1969

Beth Chatto Gardens

Location: Elmstead Market, Essex
Designed by: Beth Chatto
Created: 1960 onwards

When Beth Chatto (1923–2018) stopped exhibiting at the Chelsea Flower Show in 1987 after winning ten Gold Medals, it might have seemed that her career as a plantswoman had peaked. She had already published three bestselling books and run her nursery since 1967.

However, no longer having to plan for Chelsea enabled her to turn her focus back to her gardens on a 12-acre (4.86ha) site at Elmstead Market, six miles east of Colchester. The already established Damp Garden was added to with the Woodland Garden. But her biggest triumph was the now world-famous Gravel Garden, planted on the site of the former car park in 1991–92, and never watered. Chatto was ahead of her time in realising that climate change would force gardeners to re-think their habits. She was the first to promote the concept of 'right plant, right place'. The Gardens and Nursery remain a magnet for lovers of unusual plants.

Catherine Horwood

Eggborough
Power Station

Location: Goole, North Yorkshire
Designed by: Brenda Colvin
Created: 1961–73

Brenda Colvin designed the landscape setting of several of the huge coal-fired power stations that were built in the 1950s and 1960s. Perhaps the best preserved is Eggborough where her landscape is outlasting coal-based energy generation. Her approach was to surround the site with extensive linear woods and mounding, both to balance the vertical height and mass of the huge buildings and to screen more unsightly lower elements such as coal storage heaps. At Eggborough these woodlands are 0.9 miles (1.5km) wide, three times the width of the giant power station and partly following the railway 1.55 miles (2.5km) long, laid out to a pattern resembling an abstract picture. In later phases within the site areas of new parkland landscape have been created for recreation of the employees and as habitat for wildlife, using soils conserved from below the structures.

Hal Moggridge

West Burton Power Station

Location: West Burton, Nottinghamshire
Designed by: Rex Savidge and John Gelsthorpe of Architects' Design Group
Created: 1961–69

West Burton represented a dynamic attempt to consider the visual impact of a power station in its design and siting, radically attempting to 'naturalise' this very modern development within the flat, rural landscape of the Trent Valley. The cooling towers were grouped at either end of the station to avoid the tendency for them to visually coalesce and impose their bulk on the surrounding landscape. Some were coloured in various shades of grey to provide a tonal contrast to their neighbours. More daringly still, yellow was used for one slightly offset tower, creating a point of reference from multiple viewpoints around which the station could articulate and cohere. As such, West Burton can be considered as a key example of Nikolaus Pevsner's post-war argument for the use of picturesque principles as a modern concern, where a new power station could be organised within a landscape, rather than being idealised or excluded altogether.

Ian Waites

Scammonden Water and M62

Location: West Yorkshire
Designed by: J. Brian Blayney, James A. Gaffney (county engineer), with Rofe, Kennard & Lapworth and Bill Jollans; J.A. Strubbe (architect)
Created: 1964–71 (designed 1962)

Leading landscape architects were quick to condemn the first section of the M1 for Owen Williams's heavy bridges and a clutter of ornamental trees more suited to a garden suburb.

Very different was Britain's highest motorway, the M62 that rises to 1,220ft (372m) on the Lancashire/Yorkshire border. Huddersfield wanted to build a reservoir in the Deanhead Valley, and uniquely in Britain the motorway follows the top of the dam. The sublime landscape is left open, with wide cuttings and wire mesh fencing to prevent snow drifts. The elegant Scammonden Bridge boasts the largest fixed arch in Britain, and Strubbe's reservoir valve tower is distinctive. Excavated peat was tipped across the moorland to soften the new contours. Further east, the carriageways separate around Wilde's Farm to avoid a fault – not because the owner would not sell.

Blayney specialised in landscaping dams, having already worked on Dove Stone dam in the Peak District.

Elain Harwood

133

Commonwealth Institute

Location: Kensington High Street, Kensington, London
Designed by: Robert Matthew Johnson-Marshall & Partners (RMJM) and Sylvia Crowe
Created: 1962
Registered: Grade II but demolished

Using ingenuity and a simple palette of materials, RMJM and Crowe created an experience that transcended their restricted budget. Broad planes of concrete paving, with elegantly thin railings, stepped up from the street, announcing the building's purpose with flags of all the Commonwealth nations. The entrance was approached, thrillingly, across a pool, whose base was painted black to better reflect the sky and existing trees in Holland Park. Sloping weirs enhanced the illusion of height, adding flashes of light and the subtle sound of trickling water. A planting bed below mature trees alongside meant you could enjoy colourful flowers, water and families of ducks as you queued beneath the hyperbolic paraboloid canopy.

This beautifully executed essay in modernist landscape was registered in 1998, becoming the first in which Crowe had a hand. Scandalously, it was de-registered to make way for three blocks of flats when the Institute was rebuilt as the Design Museum in 2012–16.

Dominic Cole

St Catherine's College

Location: Oxford, Oxfordshire
Designed by: Arne Jacobsen
Created: 1962
Registered: Grade II

Tucked away on the outskirts of the city centre, St Catherine's is on the end of an island surrounded by Holywell mill stream, the River Cherwell, meadows, a deer park, playing fields and a churchyard, all of which contribute to the tranquil setting. Here is a truly holistic design, the buildings, grounds and gardens being conceived as one interactive whole. Every detail, including the furniture and cutlery inside, and the individual plants and sculpture outside, was part of architect Arne Jacobsen's total vision for the college.

The view on approach is of linear lawns, borders and lily-filled moats that reflect the glass and concrete buildings. Buff brick terraces and walls with built-in benches give views over the river. The enclosed quadrangles between the college blocks feature shrubs and lawns divided by green walls of clipped yew. The entire effect is one of a considered juxtaposition between built form and nature.

Clare Price

Templemere

Location: Weybridge, Surrey
Designed by: Ivor Cunningham
and Preben Jakobsen
Created: 1963

Span prided itself on not just selling 'positive, modern, elegant and practical' houses, but also a new way of life, and Templemere was inspired by the Radburn principle that segregated pedestrians from motor cars. The masterplan for this new development was prepared by Ivor Cunningham in 1963 on land bought in 1961 from the Oatlands estate. Oatlands House of 1794 survives as a hotel, with grounds by Stephen Wright following William Kent, including an area between Templemere and the Thames, now overgrown with woodland.

Cunningham positioned his houses in staggered rows on the higher ground, carefully retaining existing features in the mature landscape. Instead of enclosure, he created flowing spaces that leaked out to the edges, giving the impression of continuity, while in reality the site was very confined, with 65 houses and 77 garages on 18 acres (7.28ha). Preben Jakobsen produced a revolutionary notion of artistic planting with the juxtaposition of architectural plants.

Jan Woudstra

Cranbrook Estate

Location: Bethnal Green,
Tower Hamlets, London
Designed by: Skinner, Bailey
& Lubetkin
Created: 1963

The Cranbrook estate occupies a 17-acre (6.87ha) site, formed by the clearance of terraced houses, workshops and a factory between the Old Ford and Roman roads in Bethnal Green. Set geometrically around the two diagonal axes of Mace Street are 530 homes in six tower blocks, five smaller terraces and bungalows, all arranged in a stepped sequence.

Despite the high density the estate feels open and spacious, with lawns, avenues of trees, flowerbeds and an ornamental pond making up the landscape. The pond is overlooked by Elisabeth Frink's sculpture *The Blind Beggar and His Dog*, listed Grade II*.

Inevitably the original design has been altered. Lubetkin's trompe l'oeil arrangement, visually linking the estate with Victoria Park, has been denuded and a new community centre and allotments have been added. However, the estate is well cared for and obviously loved by its inhabitants, a testament to Lubetkin's ideals, despite his later disillusionments.

Joshua Abbott

New House

Location: Ascott Road, Shipton-under-Wychwood, Oxfordshire
Designed by: Viacheslav Atroshenko and Mr Kasamoto
Created: 1964–65
Registered: Grade II*

The barrister Milton Grundy bought land at Shipton in 1958 and commissioned his friends Roy Stout and Patrick Litchfield to build him a weekend house. Their loose-knit design of Cotswold stone with monopitch roofs was allowed on appeal. They envisaged surrounding the house with a pond, and suggested John Brookes might produce a design. But then Grundy visited Kyoto with his artist friend Viacheslav Atroshenko. Inspired, Atroshenko produced a basic design and painted a mural along the western wall in 1971, but Grundy also employed a Japanese gardener, Mr Kasamoto, and the garden is a careful balance of Japanese ideas and plants below an existing canopy of mature trees. The house appears to grow out of a pool, reached across stepping stones that extend across the gravel, with rocky islands and, to the rear, a raked gravel garden inspired by the Ryoan-Ji temple at Kyoto. New House features in the film *A Clockwork Orange*.

Elain Harwood

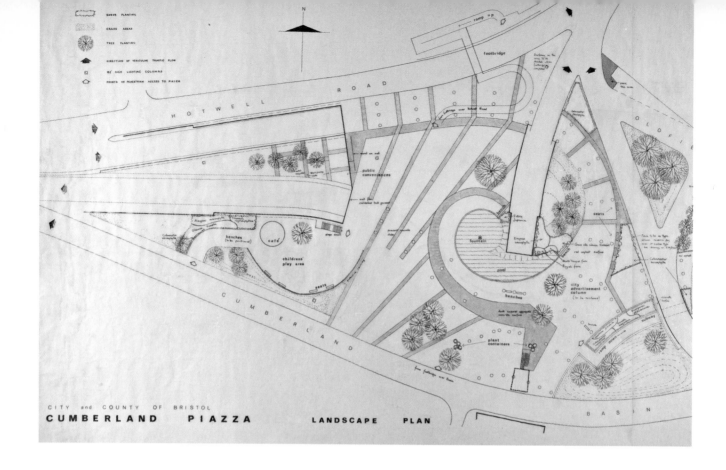

Cumberland Basin Bridges and Ashton Gate Junction

Location: Hotwells, Bristol
Designed by: Sylvia Crowe and Associates
Created: 1964–67

In 1963 Sylvia Crowe was appointed by Bristol City Corporation to design the landscape to the new roads and bridges across the entrance to Bristol's floating harbour at Cumberland Basin, linking local roads to express routes within an expanding national infrastructure.

Crowe's response to the highly intrusive engineering project was to look at the impact of the scheme within the wider landscape, with respect to views and screening. She segregated pedestrians from the fast-moving traffic by giving them separate routes, providing playgrounds for children of different ages and amenities for families. She humanised the road with 'land shaping', structural tree and mass shrub planning, and a restrained palette of modern hard materials. Norway maple, Italian poplar, lime and whitebeam have thrived and shield new buildings and cycle routes. The dynamic landscape scheme successfully integrates the functional engineering scheme into the wider landscape.

Surviving elements are at risk to potential re-development.

Wendy Tippett

John F. Kennedy Memorial

Location: Runnymede, Surrey
Designed by: Sir Geoffrey Jellicoe
Created: 1964

At the height of the Cold War, needing to demonstrate the strength of the special relationship, an acre of Runnymede and the Kennedy scholarship scheme were chosen as a state memorial to the assassinated president. Egham councillors stipulated that the memorial should be out of sight from the main road, tucked under a finger of woodland on land rising above Runnymede meadow. Within a modest budget, Jellicoe's design of paths, steps, inscribed memorial stone, seats for contemplation, and sunken fence, all set in rough pasture and woodland, remain pleasingly detailed and understated. Around this time, Jellicoe developed a fascination with the subconscious experience of landscape. His talks and writings on this project introduced invisible associations on the journey through the site, which he linked to Bunyan's *Pilgrim's Progress*. This additional layer of meaning continues to intrigue, along with 50 steps symbolising the American states and a scarlet oak, symbolising Kennedy's blood. This remains Jellicoe's best known and most highly regarded work.

Annabel Downs

West Campus, University of York

Location: Heslington, York
Designed by: Andrew Derbyshire and Maurice Lee of Robert Matthew, Johnson-Marshall & Partners (RMJM) with consultant Frank Clark
Created: 1963–80
Registered: Grade II

My memory of York is of sepia – rain clouds, mud and concrete – with the exception of Heslington Hall, the 16th-century house with its glade of topiary hedges and a pond, which were incorporated into the modern landscape created around RMJM's new university. The buildings were deliberately simple, their CLASP steel frames clad in concrete, while landscaping brought texture and colour. A central settling lake drains the flat former farmland and, crossed by five bridges, pulls the campus together. The architects devised three levels of planting: to give detail around the colleges, frame views down the lake and shield the boundaries of the exposed site.

Incongruously bright new buildings have been plonked unceremoniously into the 1960s plan and destroy the subtlety of the original colleges. Despite this, a distinctive ebb and flow of movement through the landscape endures, as every hour students leave their classes and trickle out onto the walkways and bridges.

Tess Pinto

LANDSCAPING TO THE HORIZON

When Horace Walpole wrote in the 18th century how the artist William Kent 'jumped the fence and saw that all nature was a garden' he might have described the movement from garden design to landscape architecture. In 1929 Thomas Adams had encouraged the emerging landscape profession to reposition itself, a timely move since austerity limited garden work after World War II. Welfare reforms in Sweden and America's New Deal showed how landscape could contribute to strategic planning and benefit people's lives, inspiring a series of town and regional plans to relieve overcrowding in the major cities and restructure areas previously harried by unemployment. They culminated in 1947 in a Town and Country Planning Act that provided the means for comprehensive redevelopment. Reading University had launched a course in landscape design in 1930; now in the House of Commons Ronald Tree suggested the subject deserved its own university department.

With increased post-war expectations and a rising population came recognition that pre-war development had wasted land, and of the damage done by new roads, advertising hoardings, ribbon settlements and pylons. Brenda Colvin's *Land and Landscape* in 1947 showed how our environment has been entirely moulded by man, and that our crowded island had no place for chance or muddle.

Britain's first need was for housing. In Stockholm, the director of the Parks Department, Holger Blom, had accompanied new estates with a ring of naturalistic parks, promoting woodland, meadows and water for recreational pursuits over flowerbeds. Erik Glemme produced a similar 'regional landscape' for housing at Vållingby new town, mimicked by the London County Council (LCC) at its Alton East housing estate. It chimed with the English picturesque and a reappraisal of the work of Capability Brown and Humphrey Repton, made easier by the arrival in the war of modern mechanical diggers from the United States. Faced with a real Capability Brown landscape at Alton West, the LCC recast the adjoining Downshire Field to form a flowing green valley between the 18th-century houses it incorporated into its flagship estate.

London had few large areas available for new housing. Instead, the planner Patrick Abercrombie proposed enhancing the green belt initiated by the LCC in the 1930s, and beyond it building a ring of carefully planned satellites. The Labour Governments of 1945–51 duly designated eight new towns around London, plus six elsewhere, encouraged by representations from Brenda Colvin, James Adams and Sylvia Crowe that landscape architects should be engaged there from the first.

At a conference in 1950, Crowe declared that, 'What I believe we should do is to change "Landscape in the New Towns" to "New Towns in the Landscape". We need to increase the balance of the large scale landscape, the

RIGHT Alton West Estate, Roehampton, Greater London

150

surrounding country which holds the town within its green setting, and the large open spaces which bring waves of green into the town itself, as against the sprinkling of green patches within the housing groups.' At Harlow, Frederick Gibberd had already proposed retaining broad wedges of open land along the banks of streams. Crowe showed how they could be screened by areas of woodland and willow planting requiring little maintenance, how prominent hilltops could be used as playing fields and suggested trees that could be planted in the intermediate areas of housing. She and Gibberd retained country lanes as cycle routes, along with hedgerows and mature trees, while new roads followed the contours, partly for economy. Other new towns followed these policies. Crowe also screened the industrial areas and made detailed planting proposals for individual groups of housing.

Crowe felt that she first worked on an equal footing with other disciplines at Harlow, where she was a consultant for 26 years. She also worked at Basildon, Washington and Warrington, while Brenda Colvin advised at East Kilbride, Frank Clark at Stevenage and Hemel Hempstead, Sheila Haywood at Bracknell and Peter Youngman at Cumbernauld. Other landscape specialists joined the staff of development corporations, including Bodfan Gruffydd at Harlow, Michael Porter at Basildon, Derek Lovejoy at Crawley, Paul Edwards and Gordon

Patterson at Stevenage and Wendy Powell at Hemel. Landscape architects had a very prominent role in the later new towns designated between 1962 and 1970, exemplified by Neil Higson, in turn landscape architect to Runcorn and Milton Keynes development corporations, and Rob Tregay (from 1977) at Warrington.

Enthusiasm for the new towns declined in the 1950s thanks to lower government expectations and instead turned to the better funded new universities developed from 1958, beginning at Sussex. Crowe worked at Sussex, Colvin at the University of East Anglia and Frank Clark at York.

The growing appreciation of the outdoors for walking, cycling or just contemplation had led to the formation of the National Council of Ramblers' Federations in 1931 and the mass trespass of Kinder Scout the next year. The Rambler's Association, Youth Hostel Association (founded in 1930) and the Council for the Preservation of Rural England (CPRE) campaigned for greater access to the most remote parts of England and Wales. The Labour Government finally passed legislation in 1949. First to be designated was the Peak District, in December 1950, an area whose rugged beauty was already ravaged by excavation, and where in 1929 the Hope Cement Works had opened a quarry despite fierce opposition from the CPRE. The company's chairman, Sir George Earle, in 1942 invited Geoffrey Jellicoe to produce a programme

for quarrying that set a model for future relationships between landscape architecture and industry. This was not a detailed design but a programme of intent, a pioneering methodology comparable to that of America's Tennessee Valley Authority established in 1933, which had shown that landscape management could restore an area eroded by mining and over-cropping.

Britain's post-war programme of nationalisation and industrial reorganisation saw the opening of new coal mines and power stations to supply the expanding National Grid, new reservoirs and roads. The electricity industry was Britain's biggest capital spender through the 1950s and 1960s, building nearly 60 power stations, many along the rivers Trent and Aire. In *The Landscape of Power*, a phrase used in its most general sense, Sylvia Crowe suggested in 1958 how large buildings could sit in the landscape if they were kept clean, bold and 'elemental', with no 'trivialities' in the landform or planting. At the prominent Ratcliffe Power Station overlooking the Trent Valley, built in 1964–68, Gordon Patterson showed that transformer gear and coal dumps could be screened by trees, leaving the chimney and cooling towers as landmark features.

Crowe suggested that the nuclear station at Bradwell, Essex, could be exposed to the sea but concealed on the land side, using planting to hide ancillary buildings and wires. Her discussion led to a commission in 1959 at the

LEFT Cumbernauld, North Lanarkshire (top); University of East Anglia, Norfolk (bottom)

sensitively located station at Trawsfynydd in Snowdonia, beginning a long working relationship with Basil Spence. At the nuclear station at Wylfa, Anglesey, she flanked the station with artificial hills. At Oldbury in Gloucestershire, in 1960 Jellicoe copied the surrounding field pattern, rather as in the same year he concealed the Harwell Research Station behind tree-covered mounds inspired by the nearby Wittenham Clumps. The most remarkable new hill appeared at Gale Common, East Yorkshire, where in 1967 Brenda Colvin began to make mounds from pulverised fuel ash from two power stations and a coalmine. The ash was formed into a series of terraces, then planted with grasses and shelter belts to create an artificial hill 230ft (70m)high. In 2019 some of the ash is to be re-excavated as building aggregate, and Colvin's former partner, Hal Moggridge, is advising how to retain the hill's clean lines.

In 1956, Crowe suggested in *Tomorrow's Landscape* how the expanding forestry and agricultural industries could limit their impact on the countryside. The Forestry Commission appointed her in 1963 as their first landscape adviser, after a government statement promised to make its plantings look more natural and to increase public access. Setting out a series of principles, she encouraged forest shapes to follow landforms, her sense of movement inspired by Burle Marx, and introduced a greater variety of species – particularly of native trees to balance the Commission's

fast-growing conifers – with more open spaces and picnic sites. Her work was developed by Duncan Campbell at Ennerdale Forest in the late 1970s and by Clifford Tandy and Gordon Patterson thereafter.

Landscape architects had earlier argued that large reservoirs should be met by large landscapes. Many schemes planned after World War I were completed only after 1939. Work to dam the River Derwent at Ladybower was completed in 1945, when its programme of pump houses disguised as castellated follies, sombre conifers and heavy fencing was loudly condemned by Sylvia Crowe and Kenneth Browne. At the remote Claerwen Dam in central Wales, Crowe suggested that the only planting should screen the car park when, following its opening in 1952, the reservoir became a tourist attraction.

Crowe's own opportunity to landscape reservoirs began only in the mid-1960s, at Bough Beech and Bewl Water, both in Kent. They were followed by Colliford Lake in Cornwall and Wimblehall Lake in Devon, just as the water authorities were permitting more public access for walking and fishing. She planted trees to anchor the dam into the landscape, accompanied there by some sculpting of the surrounding contours, with fingers of mixed planting along the bank to break up the view and conceal the drawdown line as well as parking. Her approach culminated at Rutland Water, where the brief demanded extensive

RIGHT Gale Common, East Yorkshire

recreational facilities. Frederick Gibberd's self-titled role as a 'three-dimensional designer' saw his firm also appointed landscape consultants to several reservoirs from the 1960s, culminating in the picturesque Kielder Water, Northumberland, begun in 1975.

The longest landscapes are those that follow roads. As early as 1939 Brenda Colvin attacked the Roads Beautifying Association, whose planting of flowering trees and shrubs along the carriageways of Britain's new trunk roads she thought too pretty. The government encouraged county councils to build more roads after 1945. Colvin was the first to complain about widening minor roads and the imposition of standardised solutions by traffic engineers, and was among many who criticised the hard, sharp lines and clumsy angles of the first phase of the MI, as well as the fussy planting selected by foresters. Though originally planned for fast cars, container lorries had the greatest impact on motorway design, because they needed gentle curves and shallow gradients. Colvin emphasised the importance of shaping a road to the contours and creating landscapes to be seen at speed, while Sylvia Crowe complained about the hard edge created by continuous fencing and the heavy lines of the early bridges. Both favoured the split of carriageways, with central reservations of varying widths, particularly on open, hilly ground. Following so much criticism, the Ministry of Transport appointed its own landscape architect, Michael Porter, in 1961, and considered the aesthetics of alignment, bridges and landscaping, planting boldly using mainly native species.

Ecological concerns were aroused in the United States with the publication in 1962 of Rachel Carson's *Silent Spring*, and in 1969 by Ian McHarg's polemical *Design with Nature*. They were followed in Britain by Nan Fairbrother's wide-ranging *New Lives New Landscapes*, published in 1970, coinciding with European Conservation Year, and its very title redolent of the new perception of landscape as encompassing the whole environment. Landscape architects turned to the reclamation of derelict land, with Clifford Tandy producing trails and sporting facilities at Stoke-on-Trent, Brian Clouston designing recreational land at Tow Law and the Centre for Alternative Technology reclaiming 40 acres (16.18ha) of a disused quarry at Machynlleth in Wales, opened in 1975.

When Crowe asked friends for their thoughts on Rutland Water, they replied 'we thought it was all natural!' Her delight in recounting the tale sums up the nebulous nature of broader landscape design – and why it needs to be better understood.

Elain Harwood

LEFT Ladybower Reservoir, Derbyshire (top); Kielder Water, Northumberland (bottom)

Turn End Garden

Location: Townside, Haddenham, Buckinghamshire
Designed by: Peter Aldington
Created: 1965 onwards
Registered: Grade II

The architect Peter Aldington always wanted to be a gardener. He and his wife, Margaret, bought a large Victorian garden in 1963 and built (largely with their own hands) three houses – one for themselves – to show how a discrete but vigorous modern design could enhance a sensitive site. Haddenham is unique in its soft 'wychert' walls of kneaded chalk and straw, and one bounds the west of the house and courtyard garden.

The original half-acre garden was 'L'-shaped, a spring garden aligned on a vista through the house and a long border at an angle offering summer colour. Garden rooms followed in 1970–76 after the Aldingtons bought more land, their more formal planting targeting later seasons. As trees have grown the garden has become shaded, save for a gravel garden (No-Mans) that has sunlight and interest all year round.

The Turn End Trust was formed in 1998 to preserve Turn End for the future.

Alan Powers

Little Sparta

Location: Dunsyre, South Lanarkshire
Designed by: Ian Hamilton Finlay
Created: 1966
Registered: Designated Landscape

Little Sparta was begun in the 1960s by the agoraphobic poet Ian Hamilton Finlay. A proponent of concrete poetry – that draws meaning from the placement of words on the page – Hamilton Finlay translated visual poetry into garden art that he placed in the valley around the small croft where he lived in the Scottish lowlands.

Collaborating with calligraphers, carvers and sculptors he created a contemporary philosopher's garden whose temples, groves, statues, urns, lochs and streams are littered with verbal and visual puns. Although the garden has no overriding theme, classical mythology, revolutionary politics and landscape painting are recurring inspirations. And Apollo – God of music, missiles and muses – is its guiding spirit. A place of culture more than horticulture, Little Sparta nestles comfortably in its rustic setting; steeped in the pastoral tradition, this provocative Arcadia sparked a fashion for 'gardens of ideas', where pretty parterres give way to witty inscriptions and arcane allusions.

Katie Campbell

Thamesmead

Location: Bexley and Greenwich,
Greater London
Designed by: Greater London Council
(GLC) Architect's Department and Parks
Department Landscape Architects
Created: 1966 onwards

Occupying 1,000 acres (405 ha) of the former Woolwich Arsenal along three
miles (5km) of riverside between Woolwich and Erith, Thamesmead was designed
by the GLC as a bold, futuristic new town to house up to 100,000 residents
and address London's housing shortage. The daring experimental design placed
concrete system-built housing among parks and open spaces. Although the
housing policy changed, much of the landscaping was completed, now amounting
to 350 acres (142 ha) of open space, five lakes and over four miles (7km) of
canals that contribute to the surface water drainage system. Some of the tumps
(moated arsenal compounds that stored explosives) have been retained and add
interesting historic elements. All these areas are now teeming with wildlife, as
well as providing much needed and valued open space and sports facilities for the
residents.

Peabody took over Thamesmead in 2014 and are leading a 30 year plan to
regenerate the town and landscape.

David Foreman and Phil Askew

German Cemetery

Location: Cannock Chase, Staffordshire
Designed by: Diez Brandi, Harold Doffman and Peter Leach
Created: 1967
Registered: Grade I

That the heathland and the scattered pine forests of Cannock Chase are reminiscent of parts of the German countryside played a significant role in the decision to site a German cemetery there.

After a treaty between the Federal Republic of Germany and the British Government, the remains of 4,939 German nationals killed in both world wars were brought here – the bodies of Zeppelin crews, sailors washed up on British beaches and those who died in POW camps. The cemetery was designed by Diez Brandi for the Volksbund Deutsche Kriegsgraberfursorge (German War Graves Commission), with the low, powerfully stark buildings designed by Staffordshire architect Harold Doffman. The dark Belgian granite of the headstones and the cover of numerous trees echo the German military cemeteries of the Western Front and stand in contrast to the white headstones and striped lawns of the Commonwealth War Graves Commission (CWGC) British Cemetery nearby.

Jon Wright

University of East Anglia

Location: Norwich, Norfolk
Designed by: Brenda Colvin (Phase 1)
Created: 1966–72

The site for the new university was the grounds of the 16th-century Earlham Hall, previously used as a golf course. In December 1967 Colvin submitted an interim report, complementing the masterplan by Denys Lasdun & Partners, who were already building on a ridge above the River Yare. Despite this belated introduction, her thoughtful approach has had a long-term influence on the university's character. She wrote that 'Areas of varied ecological interest occur on the site […] all care should be taken to conserve as much as possible of these various natural habitats'. Lasdun preferred modelling the land to planting: Colvin enhanced existing areas of Scots pines and introduced shrubs on the roadways, while Lasdun won an argument to keep the slope free of formal paths.

Colvin recommended that land by the river be excavated to form a 'broad', funded by selling the extracted gravel, and this was realised in 1975–78 roughly along the lines she proposed.

Hal Moggridge

Telford New Town

Location: Telford, Shropshire
Designed by: Telford New Town
Development Corporation
Created: 1968

Telford was designated a new town in 1968, in an area famous as a birthplace of the industrial revolution. The long history of industrial exploitation and subsequent decline had left a blighted area of disused mine shafts, derelict pools and colliery spoil. The new town would transform this unsightly mess into a 'Forest City', with a landscape plan that harnessed the vigorous shapes left by dereliction, with massive projects of earth moulding and planting. Using its own nursery, the development corporation planted in excess of five million trees, resulting in approximately 80m squared of woodland for every resident of the town. At the centre is a 450-acre (182.11ha) park, transforming flooded clay pits into ornamental lakes.

Telford was an astonishingly ambitious response to the scars of deindustrialisation. It healed but did not erase the industrial past, as places resonant with industrial heritage within its boundaries, such as Ironbridge and Coalbrookdale, were restored and celebrated.

Otto Saumarez Smith

Apollo Pavilion

Location: Sunny Blunts, Peterlee,
County Durham
Designed by: Victor Pasmore
Created: 1963–69
Registered: Grade II

Peterlee new town was conceived to provide facilities for the area's pit villages and to provide alternative employment. Berthold Lubetkin produced an ambitious masterplan but fell out with the coal board and the town's general manager, A.V. Williams. In 1955 Williams challenged the mundane growth that followed, and commissioned the artist Victor Pasmore to design layouts in its south-west sector.

Once a brief was established, Pasmore made the first sketches. He established drifts of low-rise housing and small walled gardens across the contours, punctuated by square four-storey blocks of flats and clumps of trees. In the absence of a school or church, Pasmore created a focus with a bridge-cum-sculpture covering a dam over a stream, named after the USA's moon landing. Pasmore's young architect colleagues skimped on roofing to provide better kitchens, causing leaks and leading residents to deride the pavilion in disgust. However, the Apollo Pavilion was restored in the 2000s.

Elain Harwood

Byker Estate

Location: Newcastle, Tyne and Wear
Designed by: Ralph Erskine's
Arkitektkontor AB
Created: 1969–82

Erskine was one of the first to employ a specialist landscape architect in the design of public housing. His 'plan of intent' for rebuilding Byker, approved in 1970, exploited the site's steep, south-facing slope and promised an individual touch to each group of some 250 houses. A variety of hard surfaces, grassy areas and children's playgrounds were strung through the low-rise housing set along pedestrian paths in the microclimate created by the Byker Wall to the north. Erskine established tree banks, used to shield the open car parking areas. He treated courtyards as semi-private space, protected by narrow entrances, with a bridge at Bolam Coyne, a secondary 'wall' in the south of the estate. His assistants salvaged kerbs and setts from the old streets, and architectural features from the old town hall. Timber car ports, pergolas and seats are idiosyncratic features, while carefully clipped shrubs form intricate patterns of lush planting.

Elain Harwood

Shute House

Location: Church Lane, Donhead
St Mary, Dorset
Designed by: Sir Geoffrey Jellicoe
Created: 1969–93

Michael Tree had known Jellicoe all his life, and when he and his wife Lady Anne bought Shute House they collaborated on remodelling a small, complex masterpiece. Jellicoe worked on it through the years of his retirement, while Lady Anne devised the planting.

Water dominates the garden, fed by a stream that emerges from the highest pond, which earlier centuries had used to create fishponds and a canal. Jellicoe added an exedra and sited sculpture, under which he diverted water into a rill, sheltered by beech hedges and punctuated by cascades set with tubes devised to give contrasting musical tones. At its bottom he transformed a hammer-shaped pond into a bog garden. Jellicoe returned in 1986–88 to remodel fishponds in the adjoining open field, visible from the terrace by the house. New owners John and Suzy Lewis recalled Jellicoe to Shute in 1993 to make further alterations – his last work.

Elain Harwood

1970–
1979

Queen's Park Landscape and Playground

Location: Blackburn, Lancashire
Designed by: Mary Mitchell
Created: 1970

This project transformed a formerly derelict site into a joyous yet robust landscape of gently undulating hillocks, cascading down in a series of stone steps and platforms to a winding stream. The landscape softens the austere Jespersen 12M system flats that loom behind.

Mary Mitchell made her name as a pioneering designer of children's playgrounds while working for Birmingham City Architect's Department. Her designs were influential on the adventure playground movement, and were significantly featured in Lady Allen's influential book *Planning for Play*. The zig-zagging 105ft (32m) long metal slide at Blackburn is set into one of the hillocks for safety. The materials used were rescued from the large-scale demolitions then taking place in central Blackburn, for a new shopping centre. The steps down to the water were formed from road kerbs, the toddler's playground from stone slabs from a mill floor, and the hillocks paved with setts from demolished streets.

Otto Saumarez Smith

Robin Hood Gardens

Location: Poplar, London
Designed by: Alison and
Peter Smithson
Created: 1972

At the heart of the Robin Hood Gardens estate, shielded from the heavy passing traffic, Alison and Peter Smithson conceived a scenography of two monumental grass mounds to create a spacious 'stress-free zone' between the two seven- and ten-storey concrete social housing slabs. The grass mounds were made from the rubble of tenement buildings originally on the site.

Peter Smithson designed the facade's syncopated patterns of vertical fins; Alison was responsible for the overall landscape design and detailing of the public spaces, including the circular play spaces for toddlers, and playing area for older children on the south border. Garages were discretely located at the lower level in a 'moat' and partly covered by the landscape.

The Smithsons, generally recognised for their contribution to the New Brutalism, saw their intervention as in the tradition of London inns and squares and the picturesque, of which they were avid admirers, bringing an idealistic image of an inviolable landscape into the city.

Dirk van den Heuvel

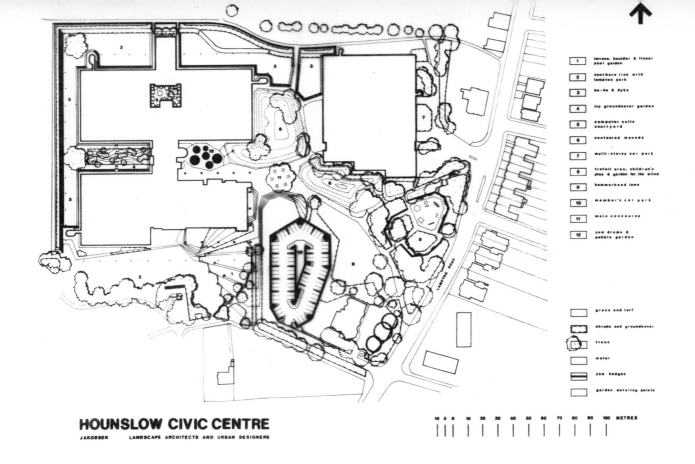

HOUNSLOW CIVIC CENTRE
JAKOBSEN   LANDSCAPE ARCHITECTS AND URBAN DESIGNERS

1	terrace, boulder & linear pool garden
2	southern link with lampton park
3	ha-ha & dyke
4	ivy groundcover garden
5	computer suite courtyard
6	contoured mound
7	multi-storey car park
8	trefoil area; children's play & garden for the blind
9	hammerhead lawn
10	member's car park
11	main concourse
12	yew drums & pebble garden

	grass and turf
	shrubs and groundcover
	trees
	water
	yew hedges
	garden watering points

10 5 0   10 20 30 40 50 60 70 80 90 100 METRES

Hounslow Civic Centre

Location: Hounslow, London
Designed by: Preben Jakobsen
Created: 1973–77
Registered: Demolished 2019

Jakobsen's design for this 12.35 acre (5ha) site expresses his love for geometry, earthworks and green architecture: modern interpretations of traditional garden elements. In 2019 the remains were destroyed for housing.

Four modernist pavilions, with interior planting by Jakobsen, are linked by courtyard gardens and surrounded by polygonal cells enclosed with yew hedges, each fulfilling a different function. Connecting paths of textured concrete lined in red brick mirrored the centre's Portland stone and brick facade. The Organic Sculpture Garden flanked the entrance: the rise and fall of green and gold drums of yew created a sense of calm, ordered assurance.

The building nestled within Jakobsen's earthworks, while the Japanese Boulder and Rill Garden, inspired by a logarithmic spiral, tapered into Lampton Park. Structured terracing was interspersed with water rills featuring stepping stones. Slabs of yew hedging formed a backdrop to sculptural perennials, ornamental grasses and shrubs, with gaps giving glimpses into the spaces beyond.

Karen Fitzsimon

Barbican Estate

Location: City of London
Designed by: Chamberlin, Powell & Bon
Created: 1962–80
Registered: Grade II*

The Barbican is a strongly integrated vision of architecture and a structured landscape of private and public space. This major project of post-war reconstruction disregarded the historic street pattern and radically redefined 'ground', creating a podium level paved with earthy coloured brick tiles. It incorporates a mix of residential, cultural and educational towers and blocks within a distinctive multi-cellular courtyard landscape that includes fragments of the London Wall. The canal responds to the rail infrastructure below ground, and is now planted with aquatics to create a central oasis. Major remodelling of the north-west podium was undertaken in the mid-to-late 1980s, as a result of water ingress. This area was replanted in 2016 by Nigel Dunnett, with a naturalistic mix of ecologically compatible planting. Significant vistas across the estate are an integral aspect of the designed landscape, reading as a series of huge interlocking spatial 'reservoirs' that celebrate living in the city.

Johanna Gibbons

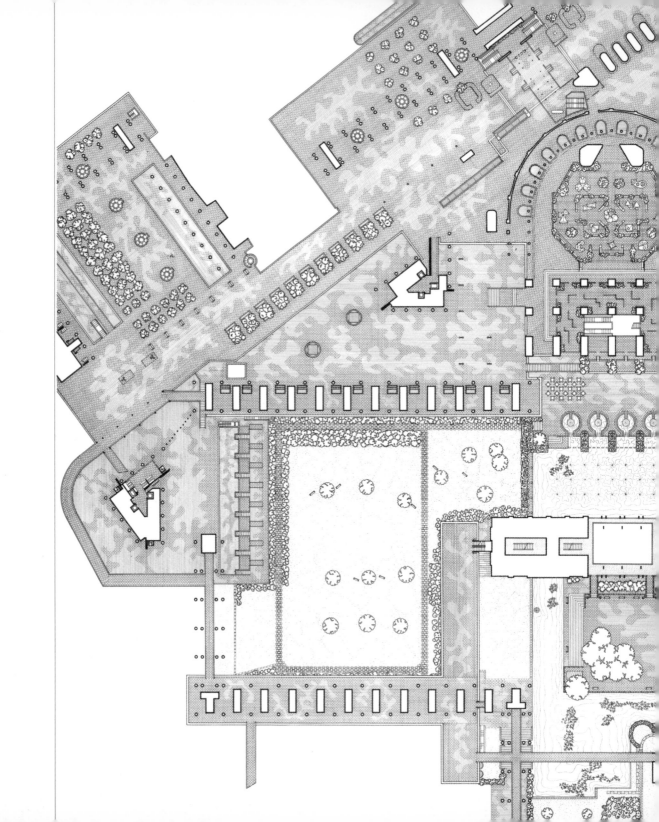

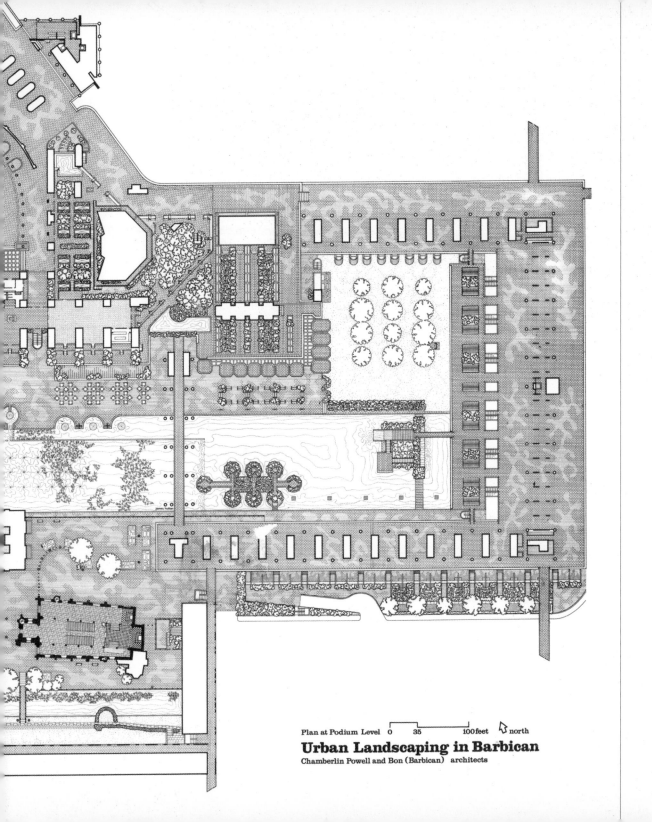

Plan at Podium Level 0 35 100 feet ⇗ north

Urban Landscaping in Barbican
Chamberlin Powell and Bon (Barbican) architects

Bretton

Location: Peterborough,
Cambridgeshire
Designed by: Peterborough
Development Corporation
Created: 1974

Bretton was one of three 'townships' designed and built following Peterborough's designation as a third-wave new town in 1967. Its layout was based on the 1929–32 estate at Radburn, New Jersey, United States that aimed to completely separate the car from the pedestrian, creating a safe, family and community-centred environment where it was possible to walk from one home to another, to the shops, or to a school without having to encounter any road traffic.

At Bretton, this resulted in an environment of quiet domesticity, meandering pathways and 'kickabout areas' with small mounds for children to climb up and to hang around. Since the disbandment of the Peterborough Development Corporation in 1988, the inception of 'Right to buy' and of the private housing association, the built fabric of Bretton has deteriorated but – on a summer's day, at least – the pedestrianised nature of the estate takes on the character of a verdant, informal urban park.

Ian Waites

Birchwood

Location: Warrington, Cheshire
Designed by: Hugh Cannings,
Sylvia Crowe and Rob Tregay
Created: 1974

In the 1960s Warrington's well-connected position, halfway between Manchester and Liverpool, made it an ideal location for a new town. In World War II an area to the east was taken over for an ordnance factory, producing munitions. Hugh Cannings, chief planner for Austin-Smith Lord Partnership, worked with Sylvia Crowe, who provided an initial landscape masterplan for the redevelopment of the area. Birchwood, the best known of Warrington's new neighbourhoods, covered some 1000 acres (400ha) and was designed as housing articulated by strips of woodland. This innovative concept for Britain was refined in 1974 by Rob Tregay, who had just finished studying in Manchester and, through his tutor Allan Ruff, had been inspired by new European ecological approaches. Tregay created the framework of semi-natural woodland that diversifies the character of the area by deliberately deploying a range of native trees and shrubs rather than fast-growing species.

Jan Woudstra

Silksworth Sports Complex

Location: Silksworth, Sunderland
Designed by: Brian Clouston and
Partners and Sunderland City Council
Created: 1974–94

Formerly a vast area of dereliction, comprising huge shale heaps that continued to burn, flooded areas and disused buildings, the site was reclaimed and transformed in the 1970s. Smoothly contoured and tree-planted slopes and mounds now enclose and shelter football pitches, tennis courts, an athletics track and lakes for water sports and fishing. A 502ft (153m) long artificial ski slope, the region's largest, sits on the highest hill affording panoramic views to the surrounding area.

The parkland setting covers 168 acres (68ha). The sports facilities were opened in the early 1980s, with more recent developments including wheeled sports, natural play, indoor tennis and a swimming pool. The clay soil was heavily compacted to lower the below ground temperatures. Hardy alders and poplars are the dominant trees. Reduced cutting regimes have recently encouraged a more diverse flora in the grassland areas. Enthusiastic runners can join the weekly Park Run on Saturdays.

Kevin Johnson

Gateway House (now Mountbatten House)

Location: Basing View, Basingstoke, Hampshire
Designed by: Arup Associates Group 2 and James Russell
Created: 1974
Registered: Grade II

Nicholas Hare of Arup Associates conceived roof gardens for the offices of paper manufacturer's Wiggins Teape, stepping the south and east facades to maximise long views and hide a busy road below. He was perhaps inspired by Roche & Dinkeloo's Oakland Museum and SOM's Weyerhaeuser headquarters near Tacoma, Washington, United States. He visited the Biba roof garden with James Russell, who drew directly onto the architects' drawings, the final plant selection overseen by Charles Funke.

There are five levels of garden, accessed from open-plan offices, the lowest level with a pond, overlooked by the largest garden on the one above. There are three higher levels, that at the top with a Japanese garden. Hare covered the roof slabs with glass insulation and asphalt, then added topsoil 225–900mm deep adding to the building's even temperatures. Stored rainwater fed into an irrigation system (now defunct). Hare's Group 2 wanted the planting to be 'romantic rather than formal' with trailing plants and climbers.

Elain Harwood

The Laskett

Location: Much Birch, Herefordshire
Designed by: Sir Roy Strong
and Julia Trevelyan Oman
Created: from 1974

The Laskett garden was created in 1974 out of a bare field by Sir Roy and his late wife Julia, expanding as funds allowed. It records the marriage and friendships of two people with a key role in the artistic and cultural life of our nation, as well as the lives of several important cats.

A garden of rooms, like Hidcote, it is underpinned by Sir Roy's research into Tudor and Stuart cultural life and Julia's experience of operatic design. An Elizabethan walk, celebrating both Elizabeths, leads from a crowned pillar to an urn: the Shakespeare Monument. One can then turn towards the 50th Birthday Garden, the Ashton Arbour named for Sir Frederick, and the V&A Temple, a platform looking back to the urn. Many other routes, the latest replacing earlier productive gardens, include one from the newly enriched facade of the house via the Fountain Court, Topiary Garden, Arts Court and Colonnade Court for events.

Charles Boot

Rutland Water

Location: Rutland
Designed by: Sylvia Crowe
Created: 1971–75

Originally called Empingham reservoir, Rutland Water was formed by damming the Gwash valley, and is fed by the Welland and Nene rivers. The Water Act of 1973 brought a duty to use reservoirs for public recreation. Crowe's brief was to make it look natural, while providing facilities for walking, sailing, fishing and birdwatching. The shallow western end is a nature reserve, managed by Leicestershire and Rutland Wildlife Trust, and the deeper eastern end is used for recreation. Crowe planted grasses, willow and alder at the lake edge to hide mudflats exposed when the level of the reservoir dropped, and screened car parks with grassed mounds and trees. Head forester Tony Ford planted 175 acres (70.8ha) of new woodland and 8.5 miles (13.6 km) of hedge. Normanton Church on Hambleton peninsula was repaired in 1983 to house a museum about the reservoir. Visitors now say that the lake 'looks as though it has always been there'.

Susannah Charlton

5 Pipers
Green Lane

Location: Edgware, Middlesex
Designed by: Preben Jakobsen
Created: 1979–81
Registered: Destroyed 2019 save for pool.

This was a rare garden design by Jakobsen, in a canon dominated by corporate and institutional projects. Client Michael Morris commissioned a Californian outdoor style garden for his family. Inspired by constructivism, Jakobsen responded by treating the site as a sculptural installation. The focal point of the south-facing back garden remains a mosaic-lined turquoise swimming pool, surrounded by slightly raised terraces, and an L-shaped, illuminated, hardwood pergola. An ornamental fishpond sits in the 90° turn of the pergola. Opposite were an outdoor kitchen, pool room, the main house and large lawn. The plot was enclosed by a cubist timber fence, while buff-coloured clay paviours emphasised the linear timber elements. The terrace was planted with a multi-level sculptural installation of glaucous flat-topped plants, punctuated with spires and dressed with a groundcover of cobbles interspersed with boulders. Jakobsen's influential Chelsea Flower Show Sculpture Garden in 1982 was based on the garden at Pipers Green Lane. Only the pool now remains.

Karen Fitzsimon

Alexandra Road Park

Location: South Hampstead, London
Designed by: Neave Brown and
Janet Jack (landscape)
Created: 1977–80

Alexandra Road Park is an innovative public park at the heart of the iconic Camden housing scheme. Its modernist integration of landscape and architectural design is unique internationally. The whole surface of the site is treated as a sculpted landscape that relies on strong geometric design, complex levels, generous planting for wind shelter and a consistent approach to hard landscape detailing to create an unusually dense and intricate park.

There is a great variety of open and closed, private and communal spaces, designed to create intimacy and a sense of mystery, and also to encourage adventurous play, to stimulate the senses and to evoke a sense of country in a dense urban setting. It is a key example of the mid-20th century approach to design, social inclusion and play. Following a campaign by residents, the park was conserved with a pioneering grant from the Heritage Lottery Fund in 2015, with Jack involved in the initial schemes for new planting and playground furniture.

Sarah Couch

197

1980–
1989

Broadwater Park

Location: Denham, Buckinghamshire
Designed by: Preben Jakobsen
(landscape), Elsom Pack Roberts
– William Pack and John Ambrose
(architect)
Created: 1982–84

An office building and distribution warehouse replaced Alexander Korda's film studios. Jakobsen was involved in decontaminating the land and in reshaping it to screen car parking and to form a great circular lawn, a breathtaking 230ft (70m) in diameter, enclosed by a 7.8ft (2.4m) tall hedge of field maple. All this was reflected in the mirror-glass facade of the raised office block.

To the north the intimate Secret Garden mimics a dry riverbed. Now overgrown, colour-themed herbaceous planting, trees and shrub laid out in curvilinear beds, were interwoven with paths of round concrete stepping stones and precisely placed granite boulders. Alcove rest areas hold curved iroko timber seats, backed by modulated metal palisades – a distinctive Jakobsen feature – that are now derelict. To the south, a wooded earth-bund screens the large warehouse and a 13ft (4m) tall ivy-clad sound-baffle wall creates an unexpected verdant walkway for employees. Thick banks of shrubs are another distinctive Jakobsen trope.

Karen Fitzsimon

Denmans Garden

Location: Fontwell, West Sussex
Designed by: Joyce Robinson
and John Brookes
Created: 1946

Originally part of the Denman family's Westergate Estate, the present garden was developed from 1946 by Mrs Joyce Robinson as a market garden for fruit and flowers on land with a gardeners' bothy, stables and coach house, adjoining a walled kitchen garden, greenhouses and farmland. She also created a 'real' garden, using innovative plant associations 'in sympathy with the whole natural scene', and in 1977 added two gravel streambeds and a dry water hole, encouraging self-seeding plants that colonised naturally.

John Brookes took over the running of the garden in 1980, developing the stables and coach house (with architect Jonathan Manser) into his home and garden design school. Following Robinson's lead in harmonising with the surrounding landscape, Brookes introduced additional native and exotic plants and developed a more organic and cohesive overall design by reshaping the grassed areas and creating a natural-looking pool with a Marion Smith sculpture (since stolen) as the culmination of Robison's dry gravel streams.

Barbara Simms

Aztec West

Location: Bristol
Designed by: Brian Clouston
and Partners
Created: 1981–83

Aztec West was one of the country's first business parks, located on the M5 north of Bristol. The landscape scheme was designed to create a pleasant working environment and to promote the new workplace concept. Planting created a distinction between segregated vehicle and pedestrian routes through the site, the centrepiece of which was a pedestrian avenue lined with London plane trees that was the same width as the Broad Walk in Regent's Park. A retained country lane created an informal route, planted with cow parsley, nettles, hedging and native trees to sustain wildlife. Other features included an outdoor gym, water gardens, space for boules, and carefully placed undulating mounds to screen car parks and phased construction. The landscaping masterfully tied together the patchwork quilt of buildings designed by different architects including CZWG and Nicholas Grimshaw. The masterplan was gradually supplemented by landscaping schemes for each development site to suit the individual buildings.

Grace Etherington

Liverpool Festival Gardens

Location: Riverside Drive, Liverpool, Merseyside
Designed by: Richard Cass Associates
Created: 1984

Liverpool is the first and best preserved of the Festival Gardens, also laid out at Glasgow, Gateshead, Stoke-on-Trent and Ebbw Vale between 1984 and 1992. Inspired by the response of Michael Heseltine, then Environment Minister, to the Toxteth riots of 1981, they were intended not as permanent gardens but as catalysts for urban regeneration. At Liverpool, a site heavily polluted by landfill and toxic waste storage, remediation and landscaping was completed in two and a half years.

Unlike the other festival garden sites, Liverpool retains a substantial fragment of high-quality landscape, despite a series of speculative redevelopments. In 2010 an adjacent residential scheme included repair of a number of the garden's features and in 2012 Liverpool Festival Gardens, including the Chinese and Japanese gardens, were re-opened to the public. Sadly the Blue Peter Dragon in the Beatles Maze has not survived, while the Yellow Submarine has been moved to the airport. The gardens are now threatened with clearance for redevelopment.

David Lambert

North Willen Park

Location: Milton Keynes, Buckinghamshire
Designed by: Milton Keynes Development Corporation (MKDC)
Created: 1970–2000

Eastern Milton Keynes is dominated by a four-mile (6.44 km) linear parkland. At its head, Willen Lake is one of five balancing lakes designed to collect rainwater runoff from the new city and control its release into the River Ouzel.

The northern half is a 'quiet lake' reserved for wildlife. On the west a sculpted landform made from construction spoil provides an elegant setting for the first Peace Pagoda in the West (Minoru Okha and Tom Hancock, 1980), its adjacent Buddhist Sangha (1988) and Zen garden of chunky gravel. The park contains two significant works of art – a turf maze by Mike Usherwood from 1984 with four bronze faces at the cardinal points by Tim Minett, and a Medicine Wheel of two concentric stone circles by Roy Littlesun with Neil Higson of 2000.

Standing serenely by the lake, the Church of St Mary Magdalene by Robert Hooke, 1678–82, acts as a reminder that not everything in Milton Keynes was built after 1970.

Tim Skelton

Mallard Place

Location: Strawberry Vale,
Twickenham, London
Designed by: Eric Lyons and
Ivor Cunningham
Created: 1984

Mallard Place was the last project of Span Developments Ltd., a company formed by Lyons, Leslie Bilsby and Geoffrey Townsend in 1956 to create architect-designed 'housing for ordinary people' in landscape settings that encouraged the development of community. On a former industrial site by the Thames, Mallard Place was completed in 1984, four years after Lyons's death, and comprises 45 houses and 57 flats and maisonettes, their elaborate architectural detailing inspired by Lyons and Cunningham's work at Vilamoura, Portugal. The riverside setting features mature trees, well-designed hard landscaping and lush planting, but unlike in earlier schemes, where the focus for community life is the enclosed green courts and communal spaces, here it is a communal swimming pool.

The development of community was encouraged not only by the design layout, but also by mandatory participation in a residents' association, that manages the communal spaces. This management programme is considered by some to be Span's greatest achievement.

Barbara Simms

Stockley Park

Location: West Drayton,
Greater London
Designed by: Arup Associates and
Bernard Ede, with Charles Funke
(horticulturalist)
Created: 1985–2010

A novel business park aimed at international high-tech industries grew out of a refuse tip near Heathrow. When Stuart Lipton took over the project he appointed his preferred architects, Arup Associates, who planned the site's decontamination and first buildings. Their masterplan in 1985 established a loop of roads around two strings of landscaped settling lakes with cascades, lined with offices and with larger lakes to the north and south. To the north they set a shopping centre and an 18-hole golf course crossed by public paths.

Arup moved six million tonnes of refuse and clay onto the golf course, mixing gravel with better clay and sludge cake to create fertile topsoil for the business park. Clipped lime trees line pedestrian routes, a nod to the formal Dawley Park once on this site and illustrated by the engraver Jan Kip in 1707. Hornbeam hedges and whitebeam trees shield car parking. The first section was completed in 1989 and later phases followed after 1992.

Elain Harwood

Prospect Cottage

Location: Dungeness, Kent
Designed by: Derek Jarman
Created: 1986

Prospect Cottage was a derelict fisherman's hut discovered by avant-garde artist Derek Jarman while scouting film locations on a desolate beach. Enchanted by the sublime site, Jarman restored the cottage and coaxed a garden – furnished only with local flora and flotsam – from the barren shingle. The front, in formal French style, has symmetrical beds filled with plants and coloured gravel; the back, in English romantic style, has meandering paths around found objects – driftwood, shards of rusting metal – vertically positioned to echo the pylons marching from a reviled nuclear power station behind. When Jarman was diagnosed with HIV, the thriving space formed a poignant counterpoint to his own decline as he turned increasingly to the garden for artistic satisfaction, therapeutic distraction and medicinal herbs. With his death in 1994, Prospect Cottage became a shrine to Jarman's defiance, courage and imagination; it also promoted horticulture as an avant-garde art form and inspired a trend for extreme gardening.

Katie Campbell

Garden of Cosmic Speculation

Location: Portrack, Dumfries
Designed by: Charles Jencks
Created: 1988

The Garden of Cosmic Speculation uses nature and the senses to celebrate new discoveries in cosmology and complexity science. It started to take form when Jencks, with his late wife Maggie Keswick, excavated a serpentine lake in the grounds of her family home on the Scottish borders. They sculpted the spoil into sinuous, contoured landforms that suggested Chinese dragons (Keswick grew up in the Far East, and her book *Chinese Gardens* of 1978 remains the best general introduction to the subject).

Since Keswick's death in 1995, the garden has metamorphosed into about 30 spaces that explore aspects of recent science, including a Universe Cascade, Quark Walk, DNA Garden and Black Hole Terrace. Wave-like landforms, terraces and lawns are combined with intricate areas of planting enhanced with sculpture, such as an aluminium double helix of DNA. The garden is open to visitors for one day a year as part of the Scotland's Gardens Scheme.

Geraint Franklin

RMC House

Location: Coldharbour Lane, Egham, Surrey
Designed by: Edward Cullinan Architects and Derek Lovejoy Partnership (landscaping)
Created: 1989

This headquarters for ready-mixed concrete conglomerate RMC takes the form of a low-rise 'mat building' of landscaped courtyards, roof gardens and boundary walls. Ted Cullinan's design uses landscaping to sensitively occupy the grounds of the 18th-century Eastley End House and to blend into the green belt.

A landscape of terraces and roofs is enlivened by a series of follies, gazebos and pavilions that reflect Cullinan's love of Arts and Crafts gardens. Playful and allusive touches include rooftop extract vents in the form of giant chess pieces from Lewis Carroll's *Through the Looking-Glass* and a lakeside belvedere that references Joldwynds, Philip Webb's lost house in Surrey. Each courtyard has a different landscape treatment. A formal, axial court adjoins the Georgian house, while narrow Fern Court incorporates a bubble fountain and granite-lined rill.

After demolition was averted by listing in 2014, Ayre Chamberlain Gaunt plan to rework the complex into a retirement community.

Geraint Franklin

Galley's Gill

Location: Galley's Gill Road,
Sunderland, Tyne and Wear
Designed by: Woolerton Truscott and
Sunderland City Council
Created: 1989–91

The site was cleared of industrial dereliction in the 1970s following the closure of the coal drops. Groups of poplar and sycamores were planted on a level grass plateau sitting above the River Wear to the north and enclosed by the cliffs of the gorge to the south.

In 1989 the park was improved to encourage general recreation and for use as an events space. Some features from this phase have not survived, and its use for events has been limited due to restricted emergency access and the site's being cut off from the city centre since the closure of the adjacent Vaux Brewery in 1999.

The dramatic setting next to the Wearmouth Bridge, the historic masonry walls interspersed with steel mooring posts, create an atmospheric and unique parkland. The recent and continuing redevelopment of the Vaux Brewery site for offices and housing will no doubt increase the usage of the park.

Kevin Johnson

1990
onwards

Pearl Centre

Location: Peterborough, Cambridgeshire
Designed by: Professor Arnold Weddell
Created: 1989–92
Registered: Grade II

This is a truly rare thing: a creative landscape designed by an influential 20th-century designer, associated with a listed commercial office building, and one that was part of the overall conception of the entire development. The design flows directly from the architecture and is deliberately functional, not just aesthetic. Its primary purpose was to provide views and space for lunchtime perambulations for staff who needed convincing that moving from central London was an attractive proposition. The design was functional in other ways too: it included lakes stocked with coarse fish for fishing, a parterre for boules and outdoor events, a physic garden and a memorial garden to complement a war memorial relocated with the headquarters. Professor Weddell's carefully integrated design survives almost completely intact, except for the introduction of a maze in place of a wildflower garden and alterations to the balustrade and parterre planting to accommodate a new entrance.

Clare Price

Stockwood Park

Location: Luton, Bedfordshire
Designed by: Ian Hamilton Finlay
Created: 1991

Bought by Luton Council in 1945, the Georgian house at Stockwood Park was demolished in 1964. New gardens were opened in 1986, and the 'Improvement Garden' by Ian Hamilton Finlay commissioned by council officer, Howard Hann.

By then, Finlay's garden at his home, Little Sparta, was internationally known for introducing learned, challenging and witty concepts using structures and inscriptions. Hann's idea of a sculpture garden evolved into a thematic landscape based on playful reminiscences of ancient Rome (half-buried column capitals, anagrams of names from Ovid's *Metamorphoses*, fragments of inscribed stone as sheep, tree-plaques and column-bases for trees) developed through drawings by Gary Hincks and letter-cutting and stone carving by Nicholas Sloan, John Selman, Keith Bailey and Caroline Webb. The supervising architect was Andrew Townsend and the master gardener Robert Burgoyne. The planting is simple, in the manner of a small 18th-century landscape garden. It is a generous, visionary and surprisingly little-known public art project.

Alan Powers

West Dean Gardens

Location: West Dean, near Chichester, West Sussex
Designed by: Gertrude Jekyll and Harold Peto; later Jim Buckland and Sarah Wain
Created: 1892, redeveloped 1987
Registered: Grade II*

The gardens at West Dean, a Jacobean house extended in 1805 and now an arts and conservation college, were redesigned by Harold Peto in 1892 for new owner William James, with a Gertrude Jekyll water garden. James's son Edward was a patron of the surrealists; he had sculptor Ralph Burton encase two trees in fibreglass in the 1970s. Edward James is buried in the arboretum on the downs, views of which dominate the gardens.

After devastation by storms in 1987, Jim Buckland and Sarah Wain redeveloped the garden, acknowledging its more public function and continuing the use of local flint. Peto's striking 100m-long pergola was restored with a new planting scheme, the woodland walk and island shrubbery beds replanted, and a wild garden developed on William Robinson's principles. The walled garden contains formal fruit and kitchen gardens, glasshouses and a cutting garden. The sunken garden has been rebuilt, expanded and planted with perennials.

Catherine Croft

Thames Barrier Park

Location: Silvertown, Greater London
Designed by: Allain Provost,
Groupe Signes
Created: 1995

Thames Barrier Park was a strategic element of the London Docklands Development Corporation's masterplan. Its location was a 23 acre (9.3ha) brownfield site, which had housed industries including a chemical works, dye works and an armaments factory. An international competition was won by a team including French landscape architects Group Signes, Patel Taylor Architects and Arup, who oversaw the decontamination work. The park, completed in 2000, was publicly funded to kick-start private investment in the surrounding neighbourhood.

The design is geometrical with a central 'green dock' in tribute to the area's heritage. Concrete walls some 16.4ft (5m) high reflect the scale of the former dockside structures. Some of the area's warehouses and mills have been converted to residential use and several of the dockside cranes preserved. The green dock provides a sheltered microclimate for a 'rainbow garden' comprising strips of coloured plants. A Pavilion of Remembrance commemorates local people who died in World War II.

David Lambert

No. 1 Poultry

Location: City of London
Designed by: Lady Arabella
Lennox-Boyd
Created: 1996

Arabella Lennox-Boyd's roof garden crowns this grade II* listed building designed by James Stirling and Michael Wilford and Partners, overlooking Mansion House in the City. The design has three elements: the first a terrace at the 'prow' – a simple design of lawns (now regrettably replaced with synthetic turf), clipped box hedges and six sandstone spheres – kept low-key so as not to distract from views of the dramatic, constantly changing City skyline. There are also two restaurant terraces with perimeter shrub planting; and a circular walled garden centred on the polychromatic atrium above Bucklersbury Passage.

If the building recalls an Egyptian temple, the walled garden encircled by a chunky pergola hung with vines evokes ancient Crete. Wisteria, jasmine, camellias, fruit trees, pink hawthorn, lavender and much else provide form, colour and scent. Lennox-Boyd saw her garden as 'an example of how these kinds of gestures can radically change the face of our cities' by introducing more green spaces.

Chris Sumner

Sphinx Hill

Location: Moulsford, Oxfordshire
Designed by: John Outram Associates, with Robert Holden
Created: 1998

For 20 years Sphinx Hill has intrigued those exploring the Thames Path. John Outram was commissioned by Christopher and Henrietta McCall to design a modern interpretation of an Egyptian revival house. The house sits broad and low, its coloured render walls and shallow vaulted roofs rising over the garden and Isis beyond. Its underlying grid extends out to the paved terraces at the front and rear, 'as if the house is built among ruins'.

Sphinx Hill's formal, symmetrical garden is dominated by the Nile, a central water channel that cascades down the sloping site across three pools guarded by pairs of sphinx. Paired yew hedges establish cross axes, breaking the garden into rooms. Defining the foot of the garden, the delta in Outram's iconographical scheme is a ha-ha of Staffordshire blue engineering bricks, like those in his Isle of Dogs Pumping Station.

Geraint Franklin

Green Bridge

Location: Mile End Park, Tower Hamlets, London
Designed by: CZWG and Tibbalds TM2 (landscaping)
Created: 2000

Mile End Park has its origin in Patrick Abercrombie's 1943 *County of London Plan* that proposed a network of linear parkways and green wedges. A linear park was finally realised 50 years on by the Mile End Park Partnership, with funding from the Millennium Commission. Attending a community planning session, Piers Gough of CZWG seized upon a resident's idea for a green bridge, spanning the Mile End Road to connect the two halves of the park.

Erected in 1999–2000, the 25m-wide bridge deck incorporates areas of trees and grass flanking a cycle route and pathway. Its curved profile and glossy yellow underbelly (hence the local nickname, the 'banana bridge') avoid a tunnel effect underneath. Adjoining shops, clad in green glazed bricks, subsidise the park's upkeep. It remains Gough's favourite project: 'I felt that I had changed something', he says. 'I also like the heroic idea of the park winning out against the road'.

Geraint Franklin

The Eden Project

Location: Bodelva, St Austell, Cornwall
Designed by: Dominic Cole (Land Use Consultants)
Created: 1998

After restoring the Lost Gardens of Heligan, Eden Project founder Tim Smit commissioned Grimshaw Architects to create a home for a variety of non-native plant species in a disused china clay pit.

The landscape is structured around a series of plots telling the 'stories of man and plants'. These feature 80 plants or crops, such as wood for building or fibres for clothing, that we interact with daily, each with its own horticultural requirements. Landscaping and plants, rather than concrete, were used to stabilise the sides of the pit. At the heart of the landscape are the two large biomes housing Mediterranean and rainforest ecosystems. Cole's design was influenced by the work of Eric Ravilious and landscape architect Roberto Burle Marx. The descent into Eden reveals the genius of a project in which the natural world has been re-inserted into a former quarry. Significantly it is the horticultural landscape that encloses and guides the visitor to their unexpected destination.

Paul Lincoln

Trentham Gardens

Location: Trentham, Staffordshire
Designed by: Tom Stuart-Smith,
Piet Oudolf and Nigel Dunnett
New gardens created: 2003–16
Registered: Grade II* (forlandscape
designed by Capability Brown and
Charles Barry)

Three contrasting new gardens have been commissioned to enhance this historic estate, owned since 1996 by St Modwen Properties and now run as a visitor attraction. In 2003 Tom Stuart-Smith reinterpreted Charles Barry's Italian Gardens. The upper Rose Garden recreated the labour intensive ribbon bedding of the 1840s. For the larger parterre towards the lake Stuart-Smith retained the Barry layout but adopted more impressionistic planting with colourful herbaceous perennials in deference to contemporary budgets and taste. Piet Oudolf created a floral labyrinth of sinuous mown paths running between beds of tall planting and coloured grasses on adjoining damp ground towards the River Trent. In 2016 Nigel Dunnett laid out a wildflower meadow in the style of his work for the London Olympic Park on the west bank of the lake. The sweeping drifts complement the newly restored Capability Brown landscape, created in 1759–80. The new gardens provide variety through the seasons, encouraging repeat visits.

Alan Taylor

Barking Town Square

Location: Barking, Greater London
Designed by: muf architecture/art for Redrow Regeneration
Created: 2006–10

This T-shaped 'square' is an integral part of a large masterplanned redevelopment and consists of the civic square, arboretum, folly wall, and arcade. Muf's priorities were to clear space in front of the town hall for civic activity, and to plant trees for shade. They worked closely with the architects of the surrounding buildings, Allford Hall Monaghan Morris, and undertook extensive public consultation.

The main paving is flamed pink Spanish granite, but the 262.5ft (80m) long, 26.2ft (8m) high arcade has black and white terrazzo tiles, referring to the grandeur of urban arcades and London's Edwardian villa front paths. The folly is completely new, but so convincing that even when it was under construction, passers-by expressed the false belief that it had already been there. Thirteen large golden chandeliers suggest the glamour of a ballroom. They are almost the only bespoke element and were designed with product designer Tom Dixon.

Catherine Croft

Dalston Eastern Curve Garden

Location: Dalston, London
Designed by: J & L Gibbons with muf architecture/art
Created: 2009

Part of Making Space in Dalston, a wider public realm enhancement project, this 1.2 acre(0.5ha) garden on derelict urban land creates an integrated ecology of the natural, cultural and the historic. The popularity of the garden and its ecological impact has grown with the imaginative way it is managed for people as well as for plants and wildlife. It is as much an urban forest as a place for horticulture, natural play, pumpkin carving, cooking, acoustic performance and much more.

The open-sided oak barn was designed and built by French artist collective EXYZT together with local young apprentices. It is managed with dedication and love through the social enterprise Grow Cook Eat, with the muscle and enthusiasm of hundreds of volunteers over the years. The project provides seating and pear trees at the threshold from which to admire the celebrated Hackney Peace Carnival Mural, painted in 1985 by Ray Walker.

Johanna Gibbons

Queen Elizabeth Park

Location: Stratford, London
Designed by: James Corner Field Operations and Piet Oudolf (North Park) and LDA Design and George Hargreaves (South Park)
Created: 2012–14

The Queen Elizabeth Park was created for the 2012 Olympic Games, which enabled the assembly and reconfiguration of an urban periphery landscape criss-crossed by major infrastructure. It was well-advertised that industry and polluted land were cleared and power lines buried, less so that valued spaces for allotments, cycling and cooperative housing were also lost in this regeneration.

The park is in two parts, North and South, each with a distinct landscape character, and different audiences as a result. South Park, designed by James Corner Field Operations, with Piet Oudolf, retains elements of Sarah Price's garden for the Olympics in 2012. It is a sociable pleasure garden and on sunny days is buzzing with East London's multicultural community. North Park is quieter, with a less diverse user group. Designed by LDA Design and George Hargreaves with wetlands by Vogt Landscape at its southern end, this is a picturesque landscape that is both technically accomplished and sustainably ecological.

Bridget Snaith

Hauser & Wirth

Location: Bruton, Somerset
Designed by: Piet Oudolf
Created: 2014

Described as the international rock star of landscape gardeners, Piet Oudolf has designed an instantly recognisable landscape for Hauser & Wirth, a breathtaking 3D swathe of wild colour and excitement. Opened in 2014, the gently sloping 1.5-acre (0.61ha) field behind the new gallery is packed with over 26,000 perennials in contoured beds. The huge variety of form and texture make the garden a delight to experience.

I visited in the thundering crescendo of high summer, and particularly enjoyed the thick billowing clusters of flowers in full bloom and wispy grasses – some as high as your shoulders – evoking the romance of an English meadow. Photographs show it as equally dramatic when plant skeletons and seed heads stand sheathed in winter frost. Oudolf Field beautifully complements the wider landscape. The pavilion by Chilean architect Smiljan Radić provides fantastic views of the gardens, the gallery buildings and a dovecot in the hills beyond.

Henrietta Billings

RECOGNISING THE VALUE OF
MODERN URBAN LANDSCAPE

The landscape of the city is often taken for granted. This is perhaps because it is not obvious where landscape begins and ends, since it forms part of the wider public realm and is a backdrop to everyday life.

There are very few post-war designed landscapes on Historic England's Register of Parks and Gardens, yet the conservation charities are aware of the need to protect our recent urban landscape legacy. People too often associate only age with heritage. Recent landscapes require scholarly research to define their special qualities – either as early or distinctive examples of a style or type of landscape, to identify their importance in the oeuvre of a significant designer, or their association with a listed building or historic event – for them to be considered for inclusion on the Register. Hard elements, rather than planting (save in arboreta or special collections) are key to these decisions, say Historic England. Assessing these qualities may be challenging, since landscapes can be eroded by multiple small incremental changes. Many more are lost through unsympathetic interventions or redevelopment before they are properly recorded, simply because the people who use or look after them do not understand what makes them special and important.

Another challenge is the range of modern landscapes, whether the setting for a Grade I listed building such as Coventry Cathedral, housing such as the Alexandra Road Estate in Camden, London, a new town such as Harlow, or a large-scale landscape infrastructure such as Trawsfynydd Power Station, set within the Snowdonia National Park in Wales. Not all can be easily drawn on a map, one reason why more easily defined urban landscapes are so important. Another is that they can be enjoyed by so many people. The modern landscape is so much more than the bits in between buildings; it contributes seamlessly to the fundamental concept of a development. Over time it becomes an intrinsic and dynamic part of the identity of a community and sense of place that encompasses biodiversity as much as the built landscape.

A city is constantly in a state of flux. Landscapes do not stand still and need resources, protection and knowledge to retain the spirit of their original intent, as well as ongoing care and a careful choice of modern materials and planting that are appropriate to avoid diluting the value of the place. The modern designed landscape is particularly vulnerable because it was common for the landscape architect to express his or her intentions in no more than a sketch, roughed out in close association with the architect. This was the way that Sylvia Crowe and Peter Youngman often worked, for example. It was rapid, persuasive and effective.

The Commonwealth Institute is a case in point. With planting contributed by Crowe to a scheme by Maurice Lee of the architects Robert Matthew, Johnson-Marshall

& Partners (RMJM), this iconic modern landscape was composed of a forest of flagpoles in a field of pre-cast concrete paving crossed by an expanse of water and with a bridge leading to the entrance. Every child that visited it in the 1960s remembers the sense of anticipation and excitement it gave. It felt unusual at the time, with clean lines, intersecting geometries and a fresh, confident air. The landscape created a breathing space to gather in off the street and room enough to admire the elegant parabolic roofline. In the end, with the whole site on English Heritage's Heritage at Risk Register, saving the landscape was pitted against saving the building when in fact the two were part of the same brushstroke. In the event, both were sacrificed, with only the parabolic roof surviving.

Three of the modern urban landscapes that J & L Gibbons have been involved in restoring over the last three decades demonstrate some of the issues that they face.

Firstly, the Barbican. We collaborated with Avanti Architects in drawing up management guidelines for the Grade II* registered landscape, considering the potential impact of any works that could affect the estate's character and significance. As much a landscape as a building – indeed it is England's largest listed building, covering 37 acres (15ha) of the City of London – the vast expanses of earthy, brown clay tiles on the podium radically redefined what constitutes ground level. The landscape guidelines were the last of a series covering the estate to be produced.

The architects Chamberlin, Powell & Bon developed a distinctive multi-cellular courtyard landscape at the Barbican that is now mature. In the mid-to-late 1980s, the north-west podium had been substantially re-landscaped by Building Design Partnership, which substantially increased the area of planting. The whole area was completely remodelled in 2016 by Nigel Dunnett. This is quite beautiful in its own right and many would say it represents an enhancement of the original, but it could not be further from the original architectural concept.

The little park at the heart of the bold housing development of the Alexandra Road Estate is another example of interlocking landscape and architecture. It was also a prototype of an innovative concept of parkland and play topography, that we recently restored with Heritage Lottery Funding. We were fortunate that its authors were then still alive. The landscape architect Janet Jack and architect Neave Brown were delighted to be engaged in the process, alongside residents who had lived in the scheme since it was built and who had brought up their families in what was deemed a revolutionary style of living. They were keen to take advantage of opportunities to improve access, the quality of materials and management, which perhaps had not been possible in the early 1970s when the scheme was originally designed and realised.

LEFT The Barbican Estate, London

These two examples are integrated visions of building and landscape, reinforcing the view that heritage is at the heart of good place-making, rooted in community values. Another modern landscape is the setting of Coventry Cathedral, otherwise known as the Hill Top and Cathedral Precinct, a conservation area but not a registered landscape. With funding from the Getty Foundation, a Conservation Management Plan is being prepared for the first time since the new cathedral was built. It comes at a critical time, since the landscape seems to have been overlooked, and changes made by different stakeholders without any overarching plan are causing it to be eroded incrementally.

The landscape setting for the Grade I listed Coventry Cathedral is an ancient place that retains most of its medieval street pattern. Above is a unique skyline of three spires, while below lurk archaeological deposits of great complexity. The blitz of 14 November 1945 had a seismic impact on the local community and the nation. In his vision for the new cathedral Basil Spence embraced not just the surviving spire but the whole landscape of the ruins, by setting his basilica at 90 degrees to the original. These two critical moves create the landscape of the hilltop that can be appreciated today. The approach through a monumental porch gives a rich spatial experience, the two projecting chapels embellish the townscape, while elegant flights of steps with cantilevered viewing platforms negotiate the hilltop topography, lawns and interwoven medieval cobbled lanes, mature trees, framed views and open vistas.

Spence's approach to the landscape is articulated through studies and perspectives, and recorded in a conversation held in 1961 with Peter Youngman. He took a careful approach to retaining existing trees and creating new plantings, so that today it feels as if the landscape has always been there. However, the cumulative impact of many small, poor decisions in the everyday management of the cathedral landscape and the surrounding public realm is in danger of undermining the experience. Developing a conservation management plan is therefore a timely call for action to reinforce not only the importance of the overall setting of the cathedral but also to reveal the historic character of the landscape. Its aims and objectives recognise the importance of an integrated landscape strategy to harness the power of the place, the qualities of which are inextricably linked to the everyday enjoyment of this historic landmark, in 2015 voted Britain's favourite 20th-century building. It is only a full appreciation of the whole group – buildings, archaeology and landscape – and a holistic approach to managing their change through design and engagement with the community that will create a conservation-sensitive and sustainable development.

Johanna Gibbons

RIGHT Dalston Eastern Curve Garden, London

FURTHER READING

Lady Allen of Hurtwood, *Planning for Play*, London, Thames & Hudson (1968)

A.P. Anderson, *The Captain and the Norwich Parks*, Norwich, Norwich Society (2000)

Harriet Atkinson, *The Festival of Britain, A Land and its People*, London, I.B. Taurus (2012)

John Brookes, *Room Outside: A New Approach to Garden Design*, London, Thames & Hudson (1969)

John Brookes, *A Place in the Country*, London, Thames & Hudson (1984)

John Brookes, *A Landscape Legacy*, London, Pimpernel Press (2018)

Jane Brown, *A Garden and Three Houses: The Story of Architect Peter Aldington's Garden and Three Village Houses*, Haddington, Turn End Charitable Trust (2010)

Jane Brown, *The English Garden in Our Time*, Woodbridge, Antique Collectors Club (1986), revised as *The English Garden through the Twentieth Century*, Garden Art Press (1999)

Jane Brown, *The Modern Garden*, London, Thames & Hudson (2000)

Jane Brown, *Vita's Other World, A Gardening Biography of V. Sackville-West*, London, Viking (1985)

Katie Campbell, *Icons of Twentieth Century Landscape*, London, Frances Lincoln (2006)

Rachel Carson, *Silent Spring*, Boston, Houghton Mifflin (1962)

Beth Chatto, *The Dry Garden*, London, J.M. Dent (1980)

Beth Chatto, *The Damp Garden*, London, J.M Dent, (1982)

Beth Chatto, *The Gravel Garden*, London, Frances Lincoln (2000)

Beth Chatto, *Green Tapestry*, London, Collins (1989)

Thomas Church, *Gardens are for People*, New York, Reinhold (1955)

Geoffrey Collins and Wendy Powell, eds., *Sylvia Crowe*, Reigate, LDT Monographs /

Landscape Design Trust (1999)

Brenda Colvin, *Land and Landscape*, London, John Murray (1948)

Sylvia Crowe, *Tomorrow's Landscape*, London, Architectural Press (1956)

Sylvia Crowe, *The Landscape of Power*, London, Architectural Press (1958)

Nan Fairbrother, *New Lives, New Landscapes*, London, Architectural Press (1970)

Margery Fish, *Cottage Garden Flowers*, London, W. H. & L. Collingridge (1961, reissued by Batsford, 2016)

Trish Gibson, *Brenda Colvin: A Career in Landscape*, London, Frances Lincoln (2011)

Sheila Harvey, ed. *Geoffrey Jellicoe*, Reigate, LDT Monographs / Landscape Design Trust (1991)

Sheila Harvey and Stephen Rettig, eds., *Fifty Years of Landscape Design*, London, Landscape Press (1985)

Elain Harwood, *England's Post-War Listed Buildings*, London, Batsford (2015)

Gertrude Jekyll and Lawrence Weaver, *Gardens for Small Country Houses*, London, Country Life (1912, reprinted 1938)

Geoffrey Jellicoe, *Motopia: A Study in the Evolution of Urban Landscape*, London, Studio Books (1961)

Geoffrey Jellicoe, *The Collected Works of Geoffrey Jellicoe, the Studies of a Landscape Designer over 80 Years*, Woodbridge, Garden Art Press, vol. 1 (1993)

Geoffrey and Susan Jellicoe, *The Landscape of Man*, London, Thames & Hudson (1975)

Christopher Lloyd, *The Well Tempered Garden*, London, Collins (1970), Penguin Books (1978)

Sutherland Lyall, *Designing the New Landscape*, London, Thames & Hudson, (1991)

Ian McHarg, *Design with Nature*, New York, American Museum of Natural History (1969)

David Matless, *Landscape and Englishness*,

London, Reaktion Books (1999)

Russell Page, *The Education of a Gardener*, New York, Atheneum (1962)

Alan Powers, 'In search of the Caveman Restaurant', *Thirties Society Journal*, V (1985) pp.18–23

Alan Powers, 'Landscape in Britain 1940–1960' in Marc Treib, *The Architecture of Landscape, 1940–60*, Philadelphia, University of Pennsylvania Press, (2002), pp.56–79

Alan Powers, 'Il classicismo di Geoffrey Jellicoe' in Luigi Latini and Mariapia Cunico, *Pietro Porcinai: Il progetto del paesaggio nel XX secolo* (Venice, Marsilio, 2012), pp.123–142

Tim Richardson, *English Gardens in the Twentieth Century*, London, Aurum (2005)

William Robinson, *The Wild Garden*, London, John Murray (1870, reprinted 1977), Century Publishing (1983)

Vita Sackville-West, *In Your Garden*, London, Michael Joseph (1951)

J. C. Shepherd and Geoffrey Jellicoe, *Italian Gardens of the Renaissance*, London, Ernest Benn (1925, and later editions)

Barbara Simms, *John Brookes, Garden and Landscape Designer*, London, Conran (2007)

Michael Spens, *Gardens of the Mind, The Genius of Geoffrey Jellicoe*, Woodbridge, Antique Collectors' Club (1992)

Michael Spens, *Jellicoe at Shute*, London, Academy Editions (1993)

Christopher Tunnard, *Gardens in the Modern Landscape*, London, Architectural Press (1938, 1945)

Janet Waymark, *Modern Garden Design, Innovation since 1900*, London, Thames & Hudson, 2003

Jan Woudstra, 'Landscape First and Last', in Barbara Simms, ed., *Eric Lyons and Span*, London, RIBA (2006)

Jan Woudstra and Cristiano Ratti, eds., Garden History, vol.28, no.1, *Reviewing the Twentieth-Century Landscape* (2000)

ACKNOWLEDGEMENTS

C20 Society would like to thank all those who have contributed entries or photographs to this book, as well as members of the Gardens Trust and Landscape Institute who have given advice and help during its gestation. Particular thanks go to John East and Elain Harwood for taking new photographs for the book. We are also grateful to our editor Lucy Smith for her support and patience.

Josh Abbott printer, runs the Modernism in Metro-land website and gives tours of modernist and art deco suburbs.

John Allan consultant to Avanti Architects; chairman of Isokon Gallery Trust; author of *Berthold Lubetkin – Architecture and the tradition of progress* (RIBA Publications 1992, Artifice 2012, 2016)

Phil Askew director, Landscape & Placemaking, Peabody

Harriet Atkinson historian of design and culture, senior lecturer at the University of Brighton. Currently AHRC Leadership Fellow (2019–23)

Camilla Beresford landscape architect and historian, co-created Compiling the Record, a Gardens Trust initiative to list post-war designed landscapes.

Henrietta Billings director, SAVE Britain's Heritage

Anthony Blee partner in Sir Basil Spence's office in Islington

Charles Boot editor of GT News, the newsletter of the Gardens Trust

Timothy Brittain-Catlin architect, historian, reader at the University of Kent, vice-chairman of the Twentieth Century Society

Katie Campbell writer, garden historian and senior research fellow at the University of Buckingham

Susannah Charlton consultant, project manager at the Twentieth Century Society

Dominic Cole landscape architect, president of the Gardens Trust

Sarah Couch consultant on historic landscapes, conservation, horticulture and architecture

Catherine Croft director of the Twentieth Century Society

Gillian Darley historian, journalist and president of the Twentieth Century Society

Annabel Downs landscape architect, former archivist of the Landscape Institute

Tim Dunn historian and broadcaster

John East Interim local authority management and regeneration professional, currently CEO at Wycombe District Council; unofficial photographer for C20 Society and active member since the 1980s

Angela Eserin archivist of the Welwyn Garden City Trust

Grace Etherington caseworker for Twentieth Century Society

Kathryn Ferry independent architectural historian, writer and lecturer

Karen Fitzsimon Chartered landscape architect, horticulturalist and landscape historian; researching a PhD on Preben Jakobsen at University of Westminster; co-created Compiling the Record, a Gardens Trust initiative to list post-war designed landscapes.

David Foreman landscape architect and trustee, London Parks and Gardens Trust

Geraint Franklin architectural investigator with Historic England, currently writing a study of the architect John Outram

Johanna Gibbons landscape architect, founder of J&L Gibbons

Elain Harwood senior architectural investigator with Historic England, author and co-editor of the Twentieth Century Society Journal

Richard Haslam historian, whose books include a biography of Clough Williams-Ellis

Amanda Hooper senior listing adviser for Historic England, South West

Catherine Horwood independent social historian and author

Marylla Hunt landscape architect and heritage consultant

Kevin Johnson principal landscape architect, Sunderland City Council

David Lambert director of the Parks Agency, expert panel member for the Heritage Lottery Fund and former conservation officer for the Garden History Society (now the Gardens Trust)

Paul Lincoln director of creative projects and publishing at the Landscape Institute and commissioning editor of *Landscape*, the Institute's journal

Imogen Magnus designer and garden historian

Hal Moggridge landscape architect; consultant, Colvin & Moggridge

Tess Pinto former caseworker for Twentieth Century Society; PhD student at Royal Holloway researching the conservation and planning cultures of the Greater London Council

Alan Powers trustee and former chairman of the Twentieth Century Society, specialist in 20th-century British art and design

Clare Price head of casework for Twentieth Century Society

Esther Robinson Wild historic environment consultant

Linda Ross wrote her PhD at the University of the Highlands and Islands on the impact of Dounreay Research Establishment on Caithness

Sarah Rutherford garden historian, author, and landscape consultant

Otto Saumarez Smith trustee, Twentieth Century Society; assistant professor, University of Warwick

Barbara Simms course director, MA in Garden and Landscape History at the Institute of Historical Research; editor of *Garden History*, the journal of the Gardens Trust

Tim Skelton retired chartered surveyor, chair of Milton Keynes Forum, the city's civic society and joint author (with Gerald Gliddon) of *Lutyens and the Great War*

Bridget Snaith landscape architect, urban designer and social researcher; senior lecturer, University of East London

Chris Sumner architect and architectural and garden historian, who worked for the former Greater London Council and English Heritage; former chairman of the London Parks & Gardens Trust

Alan Taylor Chairman, Staffordshire Gardens and Parks Trust

Wendy Tippett landscape director, Andrew Kenyon Architects

Dirk van den Heuvel associate professor with the chair of Architecture & Dwelling at TU Delft and Head of the Jaap Bakema Study Centre, Het Nieuwe Instituut in Rotterdam

Ian Waites senior lecturer in the Department of History of Art and Design, University of Lincoln

Suzanne Waters architectural historian and RIBA Library Collections Cataloguer

Jan Woudstra reader of landscape history and theory, University of Sheffield

Jon Wright 20th-century heritage consultant with Purcell; has done considerable work with the Commonwealth War Graves Commission

PICTURE CREDITS

PP 14–15 Beckonscot Model Village, Buckinghamshire
PP 54–55 Derry and Toms Roof Garden, London
PP 86–87 Trawsfynydd Power Station, Gwynedd
PP 124–125 Byker Estate, Tyne and Wear
PP 174–175 Barbican Estate, London
PP 198–199 Garden of Cosmic Speculation, Dumfries
PP 220–221 Queen Elizabeth Park, London

INDEX